Giving Life to Vision

Giving Life to Vision

Moving the Church from Plans to Progress

Marty Guise

RESOURCE *Publications* · Eugene, Oregon

GIVING LIFE TO VISION
Moving the Church from Plans to Progress

Resource Publications
An Imprint of Wipf and Stock Publishers
199 W. 8th Ave., Suite 3
Eugene, OR 97401
www.wipfandstock.com

ISBN 13: 978-1-62032-281-9
Manufactured in the U.S.A.

To my Lord and Savior, Jesus Christ
To drink from the well is a daily gift

To the Lay Renewal Ministries family
We journey together to tell the Story

To my beautiful bride, Diana
I am so unworthy of your love

To my children, Drew and Katie
You still give me hope each day

To the reader
Thank you for your trust

Contents

Foreword

BOOKS ABOUT LEADERSHIP ABOUND. They promise to make more sense out of the way we get things done. I love to read them, if only for the reminder to simplify or just to consider the possibilities. For me though, reading these books is risky. They can make me forget why we all like the same chair at the regular meeting or the same pew on Sunday. Leaders know change is necessary and good, but most people find it threatening and unwelcome. Sometimes in my drive to take things to the next level, I neglect to help people feel permission to look up and ahead.

What Marty Guise has put together here removes barriers to change—the excuses we harbor and even dress-up in spiritual clothing. Most of us are adverse to change because of the pain included. This fact led Jack Welch to tear off all the band-aids at General Electric in his first year. In dealing with issues at church, Marty has a far more endearing approach. Whenever I interact with him, I recognize his deep burden to give congregations permission to be intentional. He urges us to keep swinging with the moving target. But keeping the church aimed at its mission does not happen by accident. A plan is required.

Some pastors operate without much of a plan as though it were a virtue. I once heard an old African-American minister say, "God ain't early, but He's always on time." God does call us into seasons of waiting as a discipline of trust. Yet sometimes inaction is only the failure to make better use of what He has already given us.

Reminds me of a light-hearted debate between two preachers. One of them claimed that a Spirit-filled message is never tied to an outline. The other one responded, "God may show up once you step into the pulpit, but He meets me beforehand in the study!" Mapping out a sermon or a three-year strategic plan does not manage us away from depending upon God. We prepare in order to line-up with God's mission, so He may work through us more and around us less.

A church in pursuit of a clear vision is not on a quest for the perfect plan and flawless system. The effort is merely to translate God's timeless charge into the present. The role of vision is a bit like the benefit of picking a fixed point in the distance as you navigate through unknown terrain. The destination itself lies beyond that point but the object helps you keep your bearings.

A well-ordered church lined up with its mission can have an effective witness beyond its walls even in the way it operates. Too often, even large sophisticated church can operate like an extended, dysfunctional family. People shuffle into their familiar roles and stay put. Maybe that is why even top-flight professionals ignore messes at church they would never tolerate in their businesses. Yes, a church community is like family, a living, breathing thing. However, healthy organisms are organized, and their order affects the way they relate to the world around.

To become more intentional is not to loose the ties that bind, trading family for efficiency. A church of any size can become far too complex and layered, in contrast to the unadorned Great Commission. In such systems, the church may succeed at all kinds of things, but with little permission to consider whether these are the right things. They need to become comfortable asking if the real, lived values of the church line-up with the core mission which God has given. They need permission to consider tough questions about whether they are organized to actually do what they profess to value.

Nothing succeeds like success, so a Biblical vision for the church can keep us from succeeding at the wrong thing. Once a church starts succeeding at the wrong thing, it can be terribly difficult to convince anyone something is wide of the mark.

Just keeping things lined up requires more intentionality than church members may realize. A few years ago, a woman joined our staff after volunteering for years. She commented later that she had no idea just how much planning and management went on even after all her volunteer hours. Churches are busy places full of competing personalities, dreams, and agendas. To keep them centered upon mission, we must care enough to be honest about their tangles, to work through those with grace, and to see past them towards a compelling vision. Marty Guise's book will help leaders to do just that.

Rev. Dr. Tim Filston
Signal Mountain, Tennessee

Preface

GIVING LIFE TO VISION is about a vantage point, yes, and biblical pictures are employed to visualize the landscape of leadership in most, if not all, churches. Yet this perspective is not just another distant description of a static religious institution. Rather, what the reader discovers here is a runway, a well-crafted ramp enabling *forward* movement.

Those entrusted with leadership in local churches are often willing to serve and expand their leadership skills. The passionate commitment of Lay Renewal Ministries has been exemplified over decades of fruit that has ripened in thousands of churches. LRM prepares the body of Christ for takeoff and propels gospel progress through unity of mind and cohesion of effort—in increments that produce *forward motion*.

You and the leadership team of which you are a part will discover illustration from situations in God's Word and practical application in the chapters of *Giving Life to Vision*. Marty Guise, passionately writes this catalyst so that your group of Christ-followers might energetically pursue Kingdom advancement into the culture where God has planted your church—for His purposes—FOR HIS GLORY!

Engaging the guiding principles and action steps set forth in the pages that follow can shift *you* into FORWARD. Experience the momentum that God brings as your church and its leaders invest *together* to participate in the commission of the Church—greatly!

Rev. Gary Bowman
PastorCare *Northeast Regional Director*
www.pastorcare.org

Acknowledgments

WHEN LRM BEGAN IN 1954, the first files were kept in a shoebox. After decades of service, there is simply no way to acknowledge the thousands of people who have been a part of what has been done. Except, as we say on every event, it's not about us. So let me praise God and give Him the glory first, last, and always!

I can say that without a few specific men, this would not have been possible. Bob Fenn, our founder, is an incredible man of God. One kind word of encouragement from him kept me going for months at a time. Joe Schluchter and Bill Wichman did so much to develop the original Interactive Master Planning material. Our stalwart Area Directors, Larry Leonard and Norris Miller, have persevered in working the fields along the east and west coasts.

Personally, I could never thank Col. Dr. David G. Hansen enough for his teaching and guiding me over the past decade. Sometimes intentionally, sometimes accidentally, he pushed me to learn more, to stretch my knowledge, and to live it out.

There have been many, many others through the Lay Renewal Family whose faithfulness and support have been a blessing from God. I thank you for being a blessing not only to me but to so many others. If I didn't put your name here and you'd like a thank you, just let me know!

Introduction

I WAS ALMOST A character in a made-for-TV movie. Looking back, I can laugh about it now, but at the time, it wasn't as amusing . . .

As a young Boy Scout, my troop was having a structured outing to help us earn merit badges. Because a requirement was to do part of the hike without adult leadership, we were split into three groups. My group consisted of my peers—none of whom had reached their teen years.

We were ridiculously lost within the first thirty minutes.

Once we realized we were lost, we began to look for some way to return back to base camp. We quickly learned that we'd been enjoying the hike but not paying much attention to our surroundings. Every tree looked like one we'd already passed—and then we realized that we had passed some more than once!

Eventually, we stumbled across an old gravel road that looked like it hadn't been traveled in at least a decade. Nevertheless, we assumed if we followed it, we would eventually reach something more substantial. We were correct and found a paved road!

However, when we did find the pavement, our group was split as to our next course of action. Some wanted to sit and wait for a car. Given our location (nowhere), that option was quickly ruled out by the majority. Some suggested we start hiking to the left while others wanted to head to the right. Others suggested we split up. Each argument began with "I think . . ."

Finally, one person stepped forward and said, "*I know we need to go that way. I'm leaving. Let's go.*" Although some weren't still sure, the group followed and we safely reached the camp.

Based on that brief excerpt from my childhood, you might think this is a book about leadership[1]. Because I don't want to mislead you, it is not. While this is a book *for* leaders, this is a book about *action*. What's the difference?

After more than five decades of ministry experiences across the United States in churches of all sizes and denominations, we have met a great number of leaders. In our desire to help leaders grow, we have read a great number of sound and inspirational books that communicated important concepts. Through *Seeing from the Summit* (2011), we sought to unite leadership principles with Biblical character models to help leaders in the church to grow in effectiveness. We believe this and many other resources are excellent tools for leaders.

> But a leader must be more than a reader.
> *A leader must lead.*
> *A leader must act.*
> *Failure to do so is foolishness.*

Now, you may be getting a little tense. Please don't misunderstand. Again, based on decades of experience in the Church, we have seen a common situation occur over and over. People are willing to be trained as leaders. In fact, many are honored by the request (or nomination) and begin the process with enthusiasm. However, this does not mean that they will step forward and actually lead—even if the church puts them into a formal position. There is a hiccup. Something is missing . . .

We won't pretend that this book will solve every issue. The only book that has every answer is God's holy and inerrant Word. If you have ears to hear, the Bible answers all.

---

1. If you'd like to read the book that preceded this, *Seeing from the Summit: The Journey to an Effective Church*, we covered the topic of leadership development extensively. The book reflects on seven Biblical character models that represented components of attitude, communication, structure and more. When that journey was finished, we had ascended to the establishment of vision.

So then, why should you invest your time in *this* resource?

Many leaders we have met over the decades have expressed the desire to have a concrete tool that presents a "*Do it!*" model for ministry. In developing what we began to call "Interactive Master Planning," we put the action areas into tangible models for implementing. This book is a resource to that end. We believe that it will help you to move forward in following God's path for your church. That may sound like an audacious hope, but it is there nevertheless.

As you begin, part one of this book will briefly set the foundation for mission and vision. If this is not firmly in place, the rest will crumble. The second part will take the concept of action areas forward and present five models from Scripture to discuss Objectives, Goals, Strategies, and Timelines and Finances. The final section of this book will carry the concepts forward through checkpoints in implementation.

The word "Church" is not a bad word. It is a divine institution given to further the Kingdom of God. The word "plan" is not a bad word either. It does not prevent the Holy Spirit from moving through the Body of Christ. Planning simply gives direction and clarity.

The key is implementation. How do leaders take the vision that God has breathed into them and carry it forward through the people whom God has called to serve?

Let's begin the journey now. May God direct each step to His glory!

PART ONE

Foundation

1

Mission

How Firm a Foundation, ye saints of the Lord,
is laid on your faith in His excellent Word!
What more can He say than to you He hath said,
to you who for refuge to Jesus have fled?[1]

The loftier the building, the deeper the foundation must be laid.

THOMAS A KEMPIS

I'll huff and I'll puff and I'll blow your house down.

THE BIG, BAD WOLF

1. How Firm a Foundation, Text: Rippon's *Selection of Hymns*, 1787.

HAVE YOU EVER HAD an opportunity to see an area after a natural disaster? I can still remember visiting El Salvador in the 1980s after an earthquake. Hillsides that once bore homes were now streaked with mud, wood and sheet metal. After Hurricane Katrina hit New Orleans in 2005, news reports carried stories and images of horrific devastation. When Haiti was ripped apart by an earthquake in 2010, the world was captivated by the resulting tragedies. Much of a city in Joplin, MO was leveled through tornados in 2011. Having driven through there many times, I could not believe the complete destruction.

Images are powerful and stirring. They stick with you. But, when I see these images of devastation, what consistently strikes me most are those one or two buildings or trees that still stand in the midst of the wreckage. Seemingly inexplicably, these things stood strong against impossible odds. How could this be possible? It reminds me of a parable.

Matthew chapter 5 begins the narrative of the Sermon on the Mount. While the precise location is unknown, it is believed that Jesus sat on a side of a hill off the northwest shore of the Sea of Galilee and taught. The topography of the area would be well suited to hearing a speaker as you rested comfortably to hear what this "new" rabbi was saying.

But His words may have sounded a bit different to the hearers. Blessed are the meek? Don't even *look* at a woman lustfully? Turn the other cheek? Don't worry? Speaking with authority, Jesus repeatedly said, *"You have heard it said, but I tell you . . ."*

When instructing, Jesus taught with rabbinical authority. He often overturned the burdensome Pharisaical additions placed upon the people under the Law. Although people weren't free to do whatever they wanted, these new concepts must have given them a great deal of things to talk about around the dinner table!

As the Sermon on the Mount concluded, Jesus said:

"Everyone then who hears these words of mine and does them will be like a wise man who built his house on the rock. And the rain fell, and the floods came, and the winds blew and beat on that house, but it did not fall, because it had been founded on the rock. And everyone who hears these words of mine and does not do them will be like a foolish man who built his house on the sand. And the rain fell, and the floods came, and the winds blew and beat against that house, and it fell, and great was the fall of it." Matthew 7:24–27

Jesus doesn't talk about the type of material used to build the houses. Jesus taught about the *foundation*. The words that He spoke were to become a part of life so that the hearer would be a strong, living testimony to those around.

IF the hearers were able to put these things into practice, to make them part of their very lives, then they would be able to stand strong in the storms of life. Sitting on the shore of the Sea of Galilee, this image would have been easily understood and gripping to the disciples.

And there was more to it than the visual image:

And when Jesus finished these sayings, the crowds were astonished at his teaching, for he was teaching them as one who had authority, and not as their scribes. Matthew 7:28–29

Jesus was breathing the Scriptures but not quoting other teachers and rabbis. Jesus was teaching with *divine* authority. Those gathered recognized there was something extremely different about this man who was now giving them instructions for life. From the very start of His earthly ministry, Jesus was concerned about setting the people on the right path for living.

We see this carried through to His last command to His apostles.

Go therefore and make disciples of all nations, baptizing them in the name of the Father and of the Son and of the Holy Spirit, teaching them to observe all that I have commanded you. Matthew 28:19–20

These words from Christ at the end of the book of Matthew are commonly called "The Great Commission" but it would be fair to call them "The Great MISSION." They form the mission of *today's* Church. It is *why* the Church exists. It is what *should* breathe life into each and every ministry.

Although it can be restated in numerous ways, the essence can be summarized as *know, grow and go.* We are to *know* Christ. We are to *grow* into Christ-likeness. We are to *go* with Christ into the world.

Can you see why the foundation is so important? Without a solid foundation built on the Word of God and the model of Jesus Christ, the Church is going to be blown about—carried by the prevailing church movement of the day.

The potential destruction is chilling.

So then, how do church leaders assure that they are moving forward on a solid foundation that is honoring to God? We will set forward five basic goals that we believe God has for the Church:

1. Exalt God

    Hear O Israel: the Lord our God, the Lord is one. You shall love the Lord your God with all your heart and with all your soul and with all your might. And these words that I command you today shall be on your heart. Deuteronomy 6:4–5

If you asked an observant Jew what the most important part of prayer is, they would most likely tell you that it is the *Shema* (*Hear O Israel: the Lord our God, the Lord is one*). Typically, it will be the first words recited of a prayer. When raising children, the *Shema* is part of the last words shared before the child is put to bed.

In an interaction in the New Testament, Jesus shares the *Shema* as the Greatest Commandment (Matthew 22: 37). We are commanded to love God. To love God is to exalt Him. To exalt Him is to praise Him. We were created to praise and glorify Him. This should establish a sense of both awe of who God is *and* humility of who we are. (We'll get to the second command soon.)

There is nothing—not one single, solitary thing—we can EVER do to reconcile ourselves to a right relationship with God. The Gift of Grace was given when Jesus Christ shed His blood on the cross. This is the only way we can have a relationship restored.

In establishing a sense of mission, leaders must first help people to understand that they were created to praise God. God must be first and foremost the focus of our attention. Someday— sinners and saints alike—will bow the knee and recognize Jesus Christ as Lord. Scripture is clear that day is coming. We don't know when. We do know that until that time, believers must exalt the Name above all names—Jesus Christ. This is our act of worship as we glorify God.

2.   Edify the Saints

> To equip the saints for the work of ministry, for build-
> ing up the body of Christ, until we all attain to the unity
> of the faith and of the knowledge of the Son of God, to
> mature manhood, to the measure of the stature of the
> fullness of Christ . . . Ephesians 4:12–13

The delicate line of "works-based salvation" versus "a faith response life-style" can be difficult to tread. Nevertheless, we are challenged throughout Scripture to live out our faith. In other words, *we do have to do when we accept what was done.*

In order to demonstrate this changed life, the church is to equip believers to develop the spiritual gifts with which God has blessed them. In a Biblical church, the Word of God must be taught and practiced. There must be a healthy prayer life—individually and corporately. These spiritual disciplines will build unity within the Body as they grow *in* Christ. It should become more exciting as people see how God will use His people! If we are willing to step out in faith, God will work through us to accomplish His purposes and expand His kingdom.

3. Evangelize the Lost

> *For the Son of man has come to save that which was lost.*
> Matthew 18: 11 NIV

One of results of a life lived out of faith is that new people may realize Jesus Christ as their Lord and Savior. God will use us when we are faithful to Him. If we step out and share the message of grace and Truth found in Christ, people may be drawn into a relationship with Him.

Churches must teach that it is the responsibility of believers to share their faith. While it may make some people uncomfortable, we are still called to share what Christ did for us. Do you know the most unbelievable part? All we need to do is share the message. Jesus paid the price once and for all. Tell the story and let God deal with the heart.

4. Engage in Life-Changing Ministry to Others

> And the King will answer them, 'Truly, I say to you, as
> you did it to one of the least of these my brothers, you did
> it to me.' Matthew 25: 40

From the Genesis call of Abraham out of Haran to the final message given through the apostle John in Revelation, God's people were set apart. They were called to be distinct. They were called to be a light on the hill. Others should see Christ through them. They should see Christ through us.

In order to do this, those who are equipped must go out in service to the world. Service (sometimes called social action) simply means that we must live by engaging others through works of faith. Jesus modeled washing the apostles' feet for us. We must engage in humble service to others—putting their needs above our own.

To repeat, this does not mean that there is ANY way a person can earn salvation. It simply reflects the response of grace in our lives by reflecting our gratitude to our God.

5.   Endeavor to Keep the Unity of the Spirit.

> I therefore, a prisoner for the Lord, urge you to walk in a manner worthy of the calling to which you have been called, with all humility and gentleness, with patience, bearing with one another in love, eager to maintain the unity of the Spirit in the bond of peace. Ephesians 4: 1–3

The final goal to be highlighted is *Endeavor to Keep the Unity of the Spirit.* Christians must do this for their own spiritual health. Gossip breeds dissension. Dissension leads to separation. Christ followers must be willing to take a stand for Truth while also seeking to achieve unity among believers.

There is something simple—*yet crucial*—for us to remember. Jesus Christ gave His life that we could be reconciled to a right relationship with our Heavenly Father. Another way of looking at it is that Christ gave His life that we might be unified with God (to the degree that our sinful human nature allows). How then can we so repeatedly fail as we seek to have unity in the Body of Christ?

Finally, keep the question of our witness to the world in your mind. If the community around us sees us arguing and fighting, they are not likely to be drawn into fellowship. However, if they see us coming together, overcoming differences and standing as one, they will be intrigued to seek to become a part of the Body. Examples of unity may draw people to the foot of the cross.

Churches that keep these five goals as the foundation of their mission will be able to make great strides in accomplishing the mission given by Jesus Christ. This should be the first filter through which all ministries and actions of the church must pass.

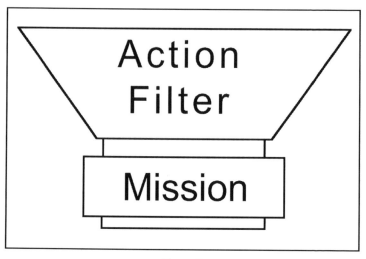

Figure 1

The imagery of a filter is something that we will begin to build as we move through the Master Planning process. A filter is something that we use to separate things or remove items that do not belong. Mission is our first filter because it defines our purpose. If something does not "fit" through the five stated goals of our mission's foundation, they do not belong in the Church as we move forward in the planning process. To be clear, that does not mean that an idea may not be good. However, church leaders must focus on that which God has called them to do. Other ministries flourish outside of the local church.

The process of creating the plan is something that should involve the entire church family. Whether it is a prayer warrior, a key leader or the pastor, there are jobs for everyone in the church. Some of the possible roles and responsibilities to begin to prayerfully consider are:

Pastor: The pastor must be intimately involved in the entire process. The pastor should be the visible champion. To be clear, the pastor should not be the main *implementer* of the process. Biblically, the pastor is called to preach and teach Word of God as the Body of Christ grows in spiritual maturity. Proper delegation of the facilitation of the Master's Plan is vital.

Ministry Facilitator: The Master Planning process will be most effective if there is a point person serving as the key link between the pastor and the church. The role of this person will be to be a communication conduit between the pastor, leadership, ministry action groups and the congregation. There will also be a need for this person to serve as an accountability agent / liaison to leaders involved in the process. It is essential that this person be able to persevere with a positive attitude and firm determination.

Leadership: The called leaders of the church are to be deeply involved in the process. Because they have been called by God into their positions of leadership, they must be committed to the process and ingrained in the development. This does not mean that there will be complete agreement on every point. That said, there must be complete consensus. Leaders must agree to go forward as the church feels prayerfully and Biblically called by God.

Key Ministry Leaders: The leaders of individual ministries in the church must have roles in the process—especially in the strategy setting capacity. They will be on the front lines of timely accomplishment of the plan in specific areas of action. They must have a passion and desire to see God bless that area with His success.

Let us now move to a discussion of the next level. In addition to knowing the foundation for our church, we must be able to discern where God has called us to go for His glory.

2

Vision

Be thou my Vision, O Lord of my heart;
Naught be all else to me, save that Thou art.
Thou my best Thought, by day or by night,
Waking or sleeping, Thy presence my light.[1]

The watershed question for many people in many congregations is:
"Do we believe our best years are behind us, or do we believe that
our best years are before us." Either way, those beliefs become a
self-fulfilling prophecy.

KENNON CALLAHAN

It would be so nice if something made sense for a change.

ALICE IN WONDERLAND

1. Be Thou My Vision; Traditional Irish Hymn translated by Mary E Byrne.

It is interesting to watch couples who are discussing home improvements. I've seen husbands and wives become incredibly irate with one another as they discussed possible upcoming changes or share about the result of a recent "update." Because the respective ideas did not line up, there were problems, hurt feelings and turmoil within the home.

And how about the church?

Is anyone foolish enough to think that the church is immune to the same problem? I hope not. Unfortunately, while we are this side of Heaven, we will continue to see people fighting for their own wills and ways.

The problem with church fighting does not typically begin with mission. Members can agree as to the purpose of the church. They see the *why we exist* aspects. But then they begin to argue about *how to fulfill* that purpose. Or, in other words, we know *why we are here* (know, grow, go) but we divide on the question of how to fulfill that purpose. In the simplest of terms, **what is our vision?**

Vision is not a discussion to enter into lightly. Truthfully, fellowship has been broken as people within the Body have argued over the color of carpets, the decorating of bathrooms and the print size on hymnals. Depending on your church experience, you may think that this is an exaggeration. You may think these things have little to do with vision. While that is correct on one level, on many others, it is an important part.

Consider this recent example. Data projectors have removed the need for hymnals or songbooks in many churches. A church with whom I consulted had an "incident" as a result. Even though they had data projectors, a group wanted traditional hymnals. That was accepted. But, as they moved forward to purchase the new hymnals, an argument began.

One side argued that money could be saved by ordering a regular font because the large print option was slightly more in cost. However, because the church had a great outreach to older individuals (who still liked the hymnal), the larger font seemed a better option since data projectors put up the song lyrics anyway. A fierce and protracted debate raged. Was this worth the fight and division? Absolutely not! Tragically, some wounds struck in the battle will continue to bleed for years. But time is not reversible . . .

Fighting does not bring the unity of the Spirit that Paul challenged the Ephesians to achieve. If there is unity in vision and a deep understanding of *why we do what we do*, the church can move forward as one. ***Vision should be the springboard built on the solid foundation of mission that will launch people effectively into ministry opportunities.*** Although we would like to make the assumption that churches at this stage of action will have an established vision, we will review some of the foundational concepts for vision. If your church does not have a current vision in place, take the time to develop it. It will be worth the effort.

Let's begin by agreeing on a working definition of vision. We'll define vision as:

> *Discerning what God wants the future to be and working to make it happen.*

While that may seem like an overly simplified definition, vision is looking upward and forward. We look upward to God and we look forward to the future. Vision requires work to develop that vision into reality.

To be clear, we are NOT in any way whatsoever promoting a "name it and claim it" approach. The past, present and future all belong to God. We are seeking His will and not our own. These three key components must factor into the vision: God's Word, prayer and understanding.

God's Word: Vision must have its roots in God's Word as leaders understand who they are and what God has called them to be. Vision independent of God is doomed to failure. In the book of Proverbs, we read the following:

> *Where there is no vision, the people perish; but he that keepth the Law, happy is he.* Proverbs 29: 18 (KJV)

You may have noticed that the King James Version was just used? Why? To begin with, this particular verse is often cited as the need for vision. While I don't disagree it sounds good and is encouraging, the Hebrew word for vision is perhaps more accurately translated as "divine revelation." Furthermore, the conjunction "but" is used to direct the relationship between the two phrases. It is to draw connection between the two parts of the whole.

So, if you'll allow me to paraphrase: *Where the Word of God is not taught, people die; but blessed are those who hear and obey!* Therefore, we **must** search and teach the Word before we proclaim God's vision. The living and active Word is God's revelation.

Prayer: The second key component of vision is found in prayer. G. K. Chesterton was known for his simple outlook on prayer:

> *Prayer doesn't change God. Prayer changes us.*

Unfortunately, because we can be biased because of personal experiences and desires, we may put our preferences first. If leaders prayerfully seek God's vision, their hearts can be united as they seek NOT what is best for them but what is best for the church. Earnest, unceasing prayer can do incredible things to ease tension, disarm hostility and bridge unity.

If your leaders and church are not prepared and willing to intentionally increase a commitment to both individual and corporate prayer, master planning will be only minimally effective. Prayer is an anchor to keep this process secure in focus.

Understanding: The final component of vision is understanding or knowledge. Specifically, church leaders must understand the particular aspects of their church. They must understand demographics of current members. They must understand the community in which the church has grown. They must understand needs, possible barriers and available resources.

For example, while meeting with an inner-city church one day, I was surprised to discover that they had a desire to become what they once were—a 1,000 plus attendance church. Because we serve a big God, this was certainly not out of the realm of possibility. Nevertheless, they also had to give consideration to the reality of their physical setting. The neighborhood had changed. The 300 seat sanctuary was surrounded by buildings. The street had little parking. Two nearby lots could be utilized but even they held limited options. Again, we don't put limits on God, but we must address issues and make plans using wisdom and understanding of our circumstances.

These three components (God's Word, Prayer and Understanding) develop the second filter in our planning process.

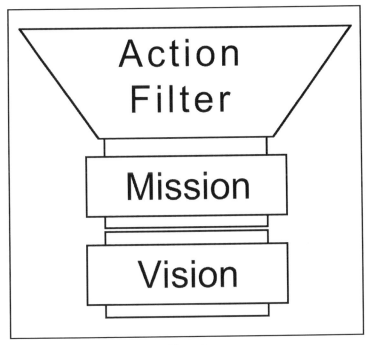

Figure 2

In order for a vision to be effective, it must be clear, concise and compelling.

Clear: Each person should be able to understand the vision simply and communicate it to others. The temptation exists to insert theological words and support it with various Biblical concepts. While this isn't a bad thing to have as support, the vision itself must be understandable by theologian and lay person alike.

Concise: The vision should be memorable. This is not a position paper. The vision should be something that people can remember. It should be something that they can repeat. If anyone asks them, "So, what is different about your church?" the person should be able to give quick highlights of the mission and vision. This is why we exist and how we are carrying out our mission.

> *Compelling*: The vision should drive people to action. If people aren't excited about the vision, they will not exert their energy to carrying it out. There needs to be a sense of urgency.

~~~

From this point on, we are going to work through the elements of master planning. Or, to be more precise, we are going to be working through the development of areas of the *Master's Plan*. We will consider elements that become the concrete ways in which the vision is to be carried out. We call these action areas.

Action areas are the areas of ministry in the life of your church towards which your energies need to be focused over the next eighteen to twenty-four months. (While it is possible to list action areas that extend farther into the future, it is best to begin with short term steps.) At the most basic level, action areas simply answer the question: *"What issues do we need to concentrate on to better accomplish our mission?"*

A wide range of people can be solicited for their insight as to the potential action areas for the church. Because the scope of areas of ministry will be diverse, many individuals may have insightful contributions as to the direction of the church. It is then the responsibility of church leaders to prayerfully seek to discern priorities and focus.

Let's briefly define the six key areas that will eventually be considerations for our action areas in the Master Plan. These areas are:

1. Needs: As the members of the church look outside the four walls, what are some of the needs in the culture and the community? What are some of the needs that have drawn people into the church? What are some of the current needs within the church? Now, how is *this* church uniquely qualified to meet those needs? What are you able to do *today* to change tomorrow?

2. Accomplishments: As we reflect back on the church's history, what are some of those things that have been especially pleasing to God? What specifically can you celebrate that could have only happened with God's Power? In other words, as you look back, what past and present successes are attributable not to a person but to *God* moving through the Bride of Christ to do amazing things?

3. Resources: How is God uniquely blessing and preparing the church today with human, physical, emotional, financial and spiritual resources? These are the tools that God is providing to accomplish His plan for your church today.

4. Barriers: What things stand in the way of our church's purpose as we plan for the future? What do we believe would stop us from accomplishing all that God has in store for us? Consider physical barriers as well as potential spiritual barriers. Lack of space is not as important as a looming theological battle.

5. Perceptions: What perceptions currently exist within our church that will help us to go forward or will cause difficulty? What perceptions currently exist outside of our church that may potentially cause difficulty as the church seeks to reach out and make disciples? Perceptions embody self-esteem and are lived out every day. Please don't make assumptions about the perceptions. Consider an anonymous survey tool that will allow individuals to honestly contribute thoughts and opinions without fear of response.

6. Dreams: What do the leaders and members earnestly desire to see happen? What are some of the unique opportunities that exist for ministry if the horizons were unlimited? It is important to be both realistic and a bit audacious at this point. The church is where it is for a reason. All too often, churches limit themselves by not considering the potential of a future with the Almighty God at their side. What can stop you if God is calling you to do something? Nothing! Don't be afraid to put forth an idea that is *only* possible through Him!

There are many ways to solicit this information from the church family. We would recommend a simple "Vision Casting" worksheet (Appendix One) that lists the six areas listed above with room for participants to write five items per section. At the end, ask them to write the top five areas in which they prayerfully believe the church should focus over the next eighteen to twenty-four months. Be sure to tell them that not everything can be done at once! Some things may fall into a longer time frame for action. These items will then be put through the first two layers of our filter.

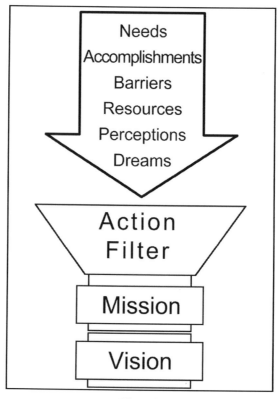

Needs
Accomplishments
Barriers
Resources
Perceptions
Dreams

Action Filter

Mission

Vision

Figure 3

Again, a filter will separate things out that do not belong together. For example, if a *dream* a person has does not fit through our five foundational issues of mission, it should not be put forward as a priority of the Master Plan.

One key element of vision MUST be accepted. God has *already* given your church everything you need to accomplish exactly what He wants you to accomplish today. Vision should not be a "When we get . . ." or "When attendance levels reach . . ." or "When we have someone who can . . ." While God may bless your church with a different vision in the future, you need to move forward from where you are.

After accepting this element of vision, leaders must agree on how to write the vision for the church. While many will quickly say that the vision is established by God speaking through the pastor, surveys cite that only five to ten percent of church pastors believe they have the visionary gifts of leadership. Therefore, the pastor must work with visionary leaders in order to seek God's vision for the church. Together, they can seek to understand how God is directing them to honor and glorify His name.

The best procedure for establishing a vision for the church will follow a pattern similar to the following:

1. The pastor and leadership of the church will set aside time to intentionally pray for God's vision. They will prayerfully read the Word while seeking understanding as to the church's and the culture's personalities. The information collected from the church family will be an important step in this part of the process.

2. Through God's leading in prayer and study, the particular elements of the vision statement will become apparent as God brings consensus to action areas. The basic elements will begin to take shape.

3. A proven wordsmith will be tasked with the role of taking the collected visionary concepts into an organized statement.

4. When the statement is written, it will be presented to the entire leadership team for approval. Following that, the statement will be presented to the church family. (Small groups may be more beneficial for gauging initial responses.)

Churches that are able to develop a clear and compelling God-centered and outreach-oriented vision will be well along the journey of the path of honoring God and fulfilling their mission given by Jesus Christ. The published vision statement will then be used as a second filter for the ministries of the church.

As leaders grasp the image of the filter, it should be clear that some things don't fit. The truth is simple. The individual church cannot—and should not—do everything. God has given you a specific vision to fulfill as part of the Bride of Christ. Let's continue that illustration in the most direct terms.

In marriage, if the husband or wife has an affair, they are doing something that does not fit within the proper and Biblical construct of marriage. This affair can cause damage that our hardened hearts may struggle to forgive. Instead of growing together, the couple will grow apart or take much time to restore the brokenness.

In the relationship between the Bride and the Groom, Jesus Christ, we know that Christ will *always* remain faithful. There is no reason to worry. However, the Bride can stray. It can drift into programmatic ministry. It can fall away from the Truth of Scripture. Some churches become hinged on the personality of a pastor or a key leader. At the risk of mixing metaphors, if that person leaves, rather than staying focused on the Shepherd, the flock scatters.

The point is simply this—any number of things can distract the Bride from faithfulness. The Church may be tempted to stray into areas that are not healthy for the relationship. It may begin with something little, but as time passes, this slight transgression becomes a major sin.

For example, some people may become upset at other pastoral or support staff because they miss a meeting or have conflicting opinions. Life is not perfect. *The focus remains on the Groom.* Another example may be an individual getting upset after hearing a sermon or a musical selection. If the worship planning team has prayerfully planned an order of worship, the opinion of one person should not become a major distraction. We must proceed prayerfully. *The focus remains on the Groom.* Leadership can work through differences in perspective because the goal is unity rather than perfection. *The focus remains on the Groom.*

The Bride *must* be focused on the Groom. As the church worships corporately and individually, each member should pray for unity in focus and ministry. The church should prayerfully consider opportunities. Some things fit. These things will become action areas. Others don't fit. While these things may become ministries for outside the church, the leaders must not be afraid to say no. *The focus is the Groom!*

The resulting outcome of this process will be areas for action.

Let us continue to move through the process of producing action plans within God's mission and vision for the particular church. We will begin with a man who "inherited" the completion of one vision and the launch of another . . .

PART TWO

Developing the Plan

3

Objectives—Joshua

You may talk about your men of Gideon,
You may talk about your men of Saul,
But there's none like good ol' Joshua
At the battle of Jericho![1]

Objectives refer to the missional direction of the church stated in a
sufficiently clear fashion that it is possible to know when they have
been achieved.

KENNON CALLAHAN

Mrs. Potato Head, Mrs. Potato Head,
Mrs. Potato Head . . . I can dream, can't I?

MR. POTATO HEAD
(WHILE WAITING FOR CHILDREN TO UNWRAP CHRISTMAS
PRESENTS)—TOY STORY

1. Traditional African-American spiritual.

IT IS A DIFFICULT challenge to assume the mantle of leadership. Unless you were the first person born (and there was only person who can claim that title!), someone was always there before you. According to those around you, the person who preceded you always seemed to do things a little differently. While you may get some reluctant but positive praise from time to time, more often than not, the former way was the "best way."

So what do you do when you are stepping into the place of someone who has lived the title of leader for the last forty years? How can you hope to "compete" with the legend that has come before?

To be blunt, you can't. The rose-colored glasses worn by those who prefer to focus on those who came before won't be easily removed. We must accept and acknowledge that we cannot compete with the past.

Following in the footsteps of Moses, a man named Joshua had an incredibly daunting task ahead of him.

> After the death of Moses the servant of the Lord, the Lord said to Joshua the son of Nun, Moses' assistant, "Moses my servant is dead. Now therefore arise, go over this Jordan, you and all this people, into the land that I am giving to them, to the people of Israel." Joshua 1: 1–2

This wasn't Joshua's first trip to the Promised Land. Remember—he and eleven other men had been sent to scout out the land forty years ago (Numbers 13–14). Ten of those men had been too afraid of the people living in the land. They would not trust in God's protection and provision to help them defeat their enemies. As a result, they convinced the people to turn their backs and that generation was sentenced to wander the desert. Joshua and Caleb were the two who trusted God. Now Joshua was chosen to lead the people into their new homeland.

But wait . . .

After forty years, Jericho was still there. The city that caused such fear was still blocking the entrance to the Promised Land. Joshua and the rest of the people had not evaded the task of doing battle with them. It was just delayed. The task remained and now Joshua had to do it without Moses. What did God tell Joshua?

> No man shall be able to stand before you all the days of your life. Just as I was with Moses, so I will be with you. I will not leave you or forsake you. Be strong and courageous . . . Joshua 1: 5–6a

This chapter is all about setting Objectives. This is not about filling in details. It's about setting the defined, achievable action areas God has given your leadership and church body the call to carry out. We're going to look at how Joshua and the Israelites embraced the objectives to enter the Promised Land, take Jericho and go forward.

Guiding Principle

In setting objectives, we seek to establish measureable checkpoints as the church goes beyond the four walls to fulfill the Great Commission.

The Challenge of Leadership

If we expect great things to happen in and through our churches, we must plan for them to happen. Leaders must be sensitive to the spiritual needs of the congregation and the community, and intentionally plan to enhance the conditions of both. As overseers of the people of God, it is the responsibility of church leaders to set and accomplish objectives.

To that end, we will consider the following questions:

- Why is it important to intentionally develop plans for the work of the church to be done?

- What is the difference between a leader and a manager?

- What comes into play when determining objectives for our church?

- How do you determine the action areas that need to be addressed in this church?

- What are the criteria for good objectives?

- How do we set qualitative objectives for *our* church?

- What are the greatest challenges when setting objectives in the church?

Setting objectives can be incredibly mundane or it can be as exciting as anticipating the birth of a child. For the church that has embraced its God-given mission and is united in purpose, the thrill of setting accomplishable objectives is an answer to a dream. Time spent on the knees reaching upward to the King of kings and Lord of lords is now coming into joyous fruition. GET EXCITED!

But he who is noble plans noble things, and on noble things he stands. Isaiah 32: 8

In him we have obtained an inheritance, having been predestined according to the purpose of him who works all things according to the counsel of his will. Ephesians 1: 11

Trust in the Lord with all your heart, and do not lean on your own understanding. In all your ways acknowledge him, and he will make straight your paths. Proverbs 3: 5–6

Why Is It Important To Intentionally Develop Plans For The Work Of The Church To Be Done?

There is a story of a pastor who would enter the pulpit of his small country church every Sunday morning and wait for God to speak through him. He did no planning or preparation. He simply opened the Bible and began to deliver the message. After years and years of this practice, he went home to be with the Lord. After entering the Gates, he expected praise for his willingness to be a vessel waiting to be filled with God's Word. However, God asked him the simple question, "Why do you think I gave you six other days in the week?"

As we begin to reflect on planning and answering the questions posed for our study of Objectives by looking at Joshua, let's look at the first few verses of this book of our spiritual history.

After the death of Moses the servant of the Lord, the Lord said to Joshua the son of Nun, Moses' assistant, "Moses my servant is dead. Now therefore arise, go over this Jordan, you and all this people, into the land that I am giving to them, to the people of Israel. Every place that the sole of your foot will tread upon I have given to you, just as I promised to Moses. From the wilderness and this Lebanon as far as the great river, the river Euphrates, all the land of the Hittites to the Great Sea toward the going down of the sun shall be your territory. No man shall be able to stand before you all the days of your life. Just as I was with Moses, so I will be with you. I will not leave you or forsake you. Joshua 1:1–5

Joshua was one of two who fully knew what the slavery in Egypt had been like. There were some under twenty at the time of the rebellion (see Numbers 13–14) who may have remembered to some degree, but Joshua and Caleb were leaders. Joshua had led the people in battle against the Amelekites (Exodus 17: 8–16). He and Caleb had braved the Promised Land with ten other men. But, because of the sin of the people, he'd been forced to travel in the wilderness with everyone else as they dealt with the ramifications of disobedience.

But now the time had come to see the fulfillment of the vision God had provided. To accomplish this vision, they had to take that first step across the Jordan River. They had to go as God was directing to defeat Jericho. They could not charge forward as they had after the rebellion and do things under their own will. Success required listening to Him and trusting in His promises. Joshua had the promise of God behind Him and, as we know, God is faithful (Deuteronomy 7: 9 and First Corinthians 1: 9).

Like the pastor in our initial story, the church that operates without taking the time to develop plans is operating as if only one day of the week matters. Effective churches determine how God wants to use them and will set objectives to assure the accomplishment of God's plan for them. No matter how sound the vision, without objectives developed to accomplish the vision, the church will drift. When you are not sure of where you are going, it is very difficult to tell whether you have gotten there or not.

If more churches intentionally determined their vision and established solid objectives to accomplish their vision, it would be astounding to see the impact it would have on the Kingdom of God. As leaders in the church, we must be setting the pace, charting the course and checking our progress. The church does not move quickly, but it must keep moving.

Remember, even while traveling in the desert, the Israelites were being led by a cloud during the day and a fire at night!

What Is The Difference Between A Leader And A Manager?

> "Be strong and courageous, for you shall cause this people to inherit the land that I swore to their fathers to give them. Only be strong and very courageous, being careful to do according to all the law that Moses my servant commanded you. Do not turn from it to the right hand or to the left, that you may have good success wherever you go. This Book of the Law shall not depart from your mouth, but you shall meditate on it day and night, so that you may be careful to do according to all that is written in it. For then you will make your way prosperous, and then you will have good success. Have I not commanded you? Be strong and courageous. Do not be frightened, and do not be dismayed, for the Lord your God is with you wherever you go." Joshua 1: 6–9

In order to accomplish the vision before them, Israel did not need a manager. Israel needed a leader.

Before we go any further, let us be clear. The world needs *both* leaders and managers. The church needs both leaders and managers. Managers are a necessary component of work and ministry. Managers at Joshua's time would have been helpful in a great number of ways. Because their skill set is more practically oriented, they would serve to fulfill tasks and complete objectives as presented by the leaders.

If we are looking for characteristics in a leader, we would look for someone who, like Joshua is bold and courageous. We would look for someone who is visionary. We would look for someone who wanted to stretch people beyond the status quo.

> And Joshua commanded the officers of the people, "Pass through the midst of the camp and command the people, 'Prepare your provisions, for within three days you are to pass over this Jordan to go in to take possession of the land that the Lord your God is giving you to possess.'" Joshua 1: 10–11

In commanding the people, Joshua did not tell them how every supply and possession had to be organized. Joshua left that in the hands of the managers. The managers were responsible for the supplies. The managers were responsible to see that the people were ready to cross the Jordan River. Joshua delegated the details as he boldly proclaimed the next step they were to take. His leadership commanded obedience because the Israelites believed in the God *behind* Joshua.

> And they answered Joshua, "All that you have commanded us we will do, and wherever you send us we will go. Just as we obeyed Moses in all things, so we will obey you. Only may the Lord your God be with you, as he was with Moses! Whoever rebels against your commandment and disobeys your words, whatever you command him, shall be put to death. Only be strong and courageous." Joshua 1: 16–18

Did you catch the end of the people's response to Joshua? "Only be strong and courageous." The Hebrew root of the word for "strong" has the meaning of "to fasten upon." A physically strong leader is impressive, but a leader fastened to God is of greater value. They'd wandered for forty years and were committed to following a leader connected to God in a way that would not be broken.

Can you see the strength a true leader brings to the forefront? Who is the leader in your church? Why do people choose to follow that person(s)? Is the "fastening" to God in that person(s) plainly visible to all?

What Comes Into Play
When Determining Objectives For The Church?

The next two questions have some overlap but again, we are proceeding deliberately through this process to insure that the leaders are unified in understanding the process. It is good to prayerfully consider the task before Joshua as a Biblical model.

Not only was he the new leader of the Israelites, he was charged to bring them across the Jordan, conquer the city of Jericho and divide the Promised Land into the allotted portions for each tribe. That's a pretty tough assignment to embrace on the first day of a new job!

But while Joshua accepted the challenge, he also stepped forward in a careful and deliberate manner.

> And Joshua the son of Nun sent two men secretly from Shittim as spies, saying, "Go, view the land, especially Jericho." Joshua 2:1a

Was it a lack of faith that drove Joshua to do this? Based on what we know of Joshua, the evidence would declare an absolute "*NO!*" to this question. But Joshua was led to get a sense of the feelings of the people in Jericho. Was it worth it? Consider the words of the scouts when they returned from their mission.

> Then the two men returned. They came down from the hills and passed over and came to Joshua the son of Nun, and they told him all that had happened to them. And they said to Joshua, "Truly the Lord has given all the land into our hands. And also, all the inhabitants of the land melt away because of us." Joshua 2:23–24

Wise leaders understand the lay of the land. They seek to develop objectives that will call the church to areas of action and ministry. They will devote prayer to the fulfillment of these objectives. They will place a priority and call for a focusing of time and energies over and above the day to day functioning of the church.

These objectives are special foci that help us accomplish the vision and assure we are pursuing the "big picture" effectiveness of God's plan for the church. Before objectives (or we can call them *areas of action*) can be determined, it is beneficial to go through a process to analyze where your church has been and where you are now. Assessing your past and evaluating your present will help you to make much more realistic decisions about your future.

In over five decades of ministry, LRM has utilized a number of different resources. Chief among these resources are surveys. The efforts that go into the study will greatly assist the church when determining objectives for future ministry. The LRM developed survey analyzes the responses of church members in comparison with "benchmarks" set by the leadership. Simple data and simple responses can lead to much more effective action. Please read the brief explanation of a simple survey we have called the *Spiritual Growth and Community Impact Survey* (SGCIS).

In 2001, LRM developed a very short and effective tool for measuring spiritual growth and outreach. Rather than a multi-layered scale system or segregated survey, the *SGCIS* was designed to be administered to your *entire* congregation annually. Two components work together to bridge leadership benchmarks and actual congregational responses.

The *SGCIS* works by asking four demographic questions and asking for "yes" or "no" responses to thirty-six straightforward statements. Thirty-one of the questions are standard. Your leaders develop an additional five "yes" or "no" questions that apply specifically to your situation. Your members will easily be able to complete this survey during a worship service in 15 minutes or less.

A second survey is administered to your leadership team. This survey asks them to consider each of the spiritual growth areas in regards to their expectations regarding the congregation as a whole. The concept is to have a snapshot of any given Sunday—during which you may have first-time, spiritually-seeking visitors sitting next to long-time disciples.

As an example, Question Five of the SGCIS makes the statement; "*On average I spend 15 minutes or more each day with God in prayer.*" In the congregational survey, the respondents are asked to answer yes or no. On the leader survey, the leaders are asked to enter a number representing the percentage of the congregation that they would realistically want to respond "yes" to this question. Again, this is intended to be a snapshot of any given Sunday and reflective of a wide mix of individuals at various points on their spiritual walk.

The analysis of the data captured using these two tools allows the creation of a Data Evaluation Report that generates significant data relating to 1) the current spiritual state of the congregation, 2) the leaders expectations in each spiritual growth category and 3) clear guidance as to where ministry efforts need to be placed. Through the creation of focused objectives for enhancing spiritual growth in specific areas, effective ministry can be accomplished. In subsequent years, as the SGCIS is repeated, growth progress will be objectively measured and compared to previous years.

By asking your members and visitors to evaluate their spiritual condition through the use of an easy to understand yet comprehensive survey, your church's progress will be easy to measure from year to year. The tool measures leadership effectiveness in nurturing spiritual growth and progress.

The *SGCIS* is a tool developed through LRM. It is not the only resource available. Consider it or another one as you are looking at various ways to evaluate what God *is doing* and what He might be calling you *to do* as you move forward under His direction.

Remember that with any survey, the intent should be to gather simple and useable information. This will then enable leaders to make practical and realistic decisions for the future.

How Do We Determine the Areas of Action that need to be addressed in this Church?

Let's tighten the lens a bit more as objectives come even more sharply into focus. Determining these areas of action requires commitment. It requires looking at the specific personality of *your* church—not the church around the block.

This reminds me of a conversation with a homebuilder several years ago. He shared some of his frustrations—good and bad—of trying to be obedient to the requests of his clients—no matter how odd those requests might have been. One of the most perplexing—and humorous—was of a woman *committed* to the use of the color purple in her new home.

The woman with whom he was working had instructed him to use a very specific and vibrant shade of purple. This purple was not just for a wall or room. It was to be used throughout the home in various ways. The builder questioned her and even ordered in some samples for her to better see exactly what it would look like. The woman was very insistent and committed to this plan. After making her sign very specific contracts, they built and painted it exactly as she requested. When they were completed with the project, they opened the home to her in great trepidation. Her response was an outburst of giddy happiness at the result! While the builders could barely stand to work in the environment, the woman was bubbling over with joy.

To put it simply, she knew what she wanted. She had a vision for a home that would make her happy. She was willing to stand strong against opposition because she had the end in mind.

As we transition to a look at God's Word, there is a passage in Joshua that is easy to overlook. Consider the setting. The Israelites are ready to move into the Promised Land. They know what they want to do and are ready to step forward. But they had to wait. Why? God wanted their obedience *first*. Part of their covenant agreement had yet to be fulfilled. Let's see what happened at Gilgal.

> As soon as all the kings of the Amorites who were beyond the Jordan to the west, and all the kings of the Canaanites who were by the sea, heard that the Lord had dried up the waters of the Jordan for the people of Israel until they had crossed over, their hearts melted and there was no longer any spirit in them because of the people of Israel. At that time the Lord said to Joshua, "Make flint knives and circumcise the sons of Israel a second time."

So Joshua made flint knives and circumcised the sons of
Israel at Gibeath-Haaraloth. Joshua 5:1–3

The Israelites had been obedient to God and crossed over
the flooded Jordan River as God miraculously gave them a dry
path. Then, as soon as the priests left the river, the waters returned. From a militaristic perspective, there was now little opportunity for retreat. The Amorite and Canaanite kings *logically*
should have attacked. Instead, they were struck with fear.

Then, Joshua made their defensive position even worse by
pausing to circumcise the Israelite men. What did this potentially mean?

Suffice it to say, a newly circumcised army would be incredibly vulnerable. In Genesis chapter thirty-eight, we read
an account of Simeon and Levi killing every weakened male in
Shechem after they were all circumcised.

But Joshua knew that this was an act of faithfulness that
had to be obeyed before they could step forward to do battle.
The Israelites had to be right with God before they could go any
further. And when the healing was complete and the people were
consecrated to the Lord, they were ready to take the next step
forward.

> And the Lord said to Joshua, "Today I have rolled away
> the reproach of Egypt from you." And so the name of
> that place is called Gilgal to this day. While the people
> of Israel were encamped at Gilgal, they kept the Passover
> on the fourteenth day of the month in the evening on the
> plains of Jericho. And the day after the Passover, on that
> very day, they ate of the produce of the land, unleavened
> cakes and parched grain. And the manna ceased the day
> after they ate of the produce of the land. And there was
> no longer manna for the people of Israel, but they ate of
> the fruit of the land of Canaan that year. Joshua 5:9–12

The model of faithfulness in Joshua is a key principle for
church leaders today. Before you can go forward, have your leaders committed themselves to following God's direction? While this

may seem like an odd and obvious question to ask, leaders must be truly centered on His will and not their own. First things first.

From this point, we can begin to determine objectives for action. As we discussed with the previous section, surveying the pulse of the congregation is a key step. When we are clear on what is wanted and sure of our direction, success in the future is greater. With this on-going evaluation, you can be assured of the continuing progress and support of your members. The body does not function well if one part is attempting to move at odds with the rest.

The broad brushstroke of objectives dictates that the following questions are answered:

- Based on our purpose statement and our vision, what are the key ministries that we should be accomplishing as a church?

- What are the ministries that we consider to be most important for our specific church?

- Which of those ministries are we doing very well?

- Which of those ministries need more of our attention and work?

- What are the unique resources that God is providing to us right now?

- What new things is He calling us to accomplish?

Based on your answers to these questions and an analysis of your current situation, objectives that require your immediate attention will rise to the surface. These objectives will become the focus for the balance of the planning process and action in the future.

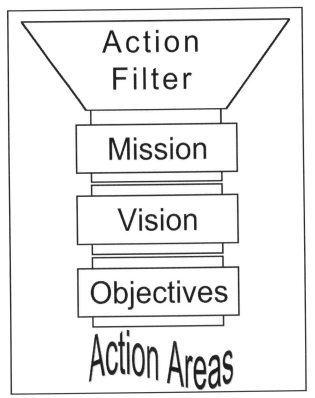

Figure 4

What Are The Criteria For Good Objectives?

As a reminder, objectives must be those "big picture" items the church is seeking to achieve under God's direction. Avoid the temptation to delve into details and stick with the primary objective.

As we see in the beginning of the sixth chapter of Joshua, God clearly laid out an objective for receiving the Promised Land to Joshua:

> And the Lord said to Joshua, "See, I have given Jericho into your hand, with its king and its mighty men of valor." Joshua 6:2

This key was established by God and the outcome was already predetermined! All Joshua and the Israelites had to do was continue to step forward in faith.

The key to church effectiveness and a healthy, vital planning process is to intelligently set objectives. The objectives should be realistic, clearly defined, reachable, desirable and measurable.

- *Realistic*—Too many church consultants evaluate churches and provide them with summary reports outlining hundreds of areas that need to be addressed. There is only so much that a church can accomplish in a given time period. The realistic church prioritizes its action areas and attacks them in an order that assures success.

- *Clearly defined*—It will be impossible for your church to accomplish its objectives unless those objectives are very clearly defined. There should be no question as to what it is that you are trying to accomplish—before you set out to accomplish it!

- *Reachable*—A church should have a good enough understanding of itself and its capabilities to know what it can do and what it cannot do.

- *Desirable*—The congregation will devote its support and enthusiasm to objectives that they desire to accomplish. It will be extremely difficult to get your people to work towards goals to which they are not committed.

- *Measurable*—You must be able to know when you have accomplished your objective. This means determining measurable results and realistic time lines. If your objective is so vague that you will not know with assurance that it has been accomplished, it is not a good objective.

Consider these two sample objectives. Do they meet the criteria?

To increase the number of new members and visitors coming to our church

To intentionally increase the opportunities for our members to share their faith with those in their sphere of influence

These objectives do not have an incredible amount of detail and strategies for implementing. That will come later. Remember, our first step is to agree on the overall areas for action. Simple and clear objectives take us one step closer.

How Do We Set Qualitative Objectives for OUR Church?

Setting objectives can seem like a simple process. It should be. For Joshua and the Israelites, the vision of receiving the Promised Land was clear. The objectives were direct. Cross the Jordan. Take Jericho. Take Ai. Proceed as God directed.

These were all simple objectives that were part of the vision. Likewise, church leaders can set direct and simple objectives under a clear and compelling vision. Let's review two words that are key to this step:

Focus: The word "focus" refers to the core aspects of the church's mission that are unchangeable. Why are they unchangeable? Because God has commanded that we must do these things. For example, a focus of the church is evangelism. When Jesus said, "Go . . ." in Matthew 28, it was a command.

Form: The word "form" refers to the way in which the focus will be carried out. The forms are flexible. For example, Jesus did not command that the only way to practice evangelism is to go out wearing blue garments and confront people on street corners. If that form works for one person, praise God. If you have a different form, then proceed with that form. We are to share our faith but the method can vary.

List the foci of your church. (Note—this is *not* a statement of beliefs. While foci should have Biblical support, they may be defined as "core values" or under another term.) This is not an exhaustive list but it should include around five to ten areas of key elements of why your church exists. (Examples: evangelism, prayer, spiritual growth, worship and service)

Now take these foci and set an objective for each. For practical reasons, we will use the focus of evangelism and an objective stated in the previous section: *To intentionally increase the opportunities for our members to share their faith with those in their sphere of influence.*

To be clear, this is NOT a time during which you will carve things into stone nor is it a time to define the "how" elements. We are starting at a basic level so the process of setting objectives is clearly understood. As we move into the next chapters, we will flesh out these objectives with goals, strategies, time lines and finances.

What Is The Greatest Challenge When Setting Objectives In The Church?

Although we may not want to admit it, the greatest challenge we can face when setting objectives is a simple, three-letter word: SIN.

> The Lord said to Joshua, "Get up! Why have you fallen on your face? Israel has sinned; they have transgressed my covenant that I commanded them; they have taken some of the devoted things; they have stolen and lied and put them among their own belongings. Therefore the people of Israel cannot stand before their enemies. They turn their backs before their enemies, because they have become devoted for destruction. I will be with you no more, unless you destroy the devoted things from among you." Joshua 7:10–12

As we learn in this chapter of Joshua, even though the Israelites had just conquered the great city of Jericho, a man named Achan chose to take some of the things that should have been devoted to the Lord. Therefore, the Israelites had to deal with the ramifications of that sin against God.

Imagine! The walls of your enemies have literally fallen before your eyes. You are in the midst of celebrating the blessing of finally entering the land which had been promised to your people. Victory is yours and even more blessings are to follow.

And yet, you steal from the One who made it all possible . . .

Sin may rear its ugly head in a variety of ways during the process of setting objectives. There may be gossip. There may be anger. There may be opposition. Why? A fearsome six-lettered monster looms on the horizon—**CHANGE!**

However, if you want your church to be different than it is today, if you want it to be more effective in reaching the unchurched, growing disciples and touching lives, if you want it to move forward under God, you must be prepared to do battle!

Change is simply one of the most frightening words in the vocabulary of humans. We like the familiar. It is "comfortable." Change is often even unwanted when people are completely dissatisfied with the current state of affairs. Churches will nearly unanimously agree that they want to challenge their people to more intense prayer lives, or that they want to attract new families to their church or that they want to dynamically increase their outreach. But, many of those same churches are unwilling to change anything in order to accomplish those objectives.

Change is a good thing when it is embraced as a catalyst to discover and implement new and dynamic methods to do the things that God wants you to do. Accomplishing new objectives to impact the church will require change. The challenge to leadership is to teach and educate those objectives to the congregation in a non-threatening way so that they will be embodied in the life rather than rejected.

The purpose is NOT to change everything (although this can be a fear). The purpose is to have effective and life-changing ministries. In the next chapter, we will discuss exactly how to develop goals to accomplish these objectives.

Leaders must be willing to do the right things for the right reasons.

Leaders must also be willing to stop doing the wrong things for the right reasons.

Action Steps

1. As a church leader (or preferably, as a leadership group), please complete this exercise to help you to focus on the remarkable blessings that God is currently showering down on your church. It will help you to isolate and prioritize concerns while targeting the barriers that are keeping you from moving ahead.

    a. List the current strengths of your church.

    _____

    _____

    _____

    _____

    _____

    _____

b.   List the current concerns of your church.

_____

_____

_____

_____

_____

c.   What are five areas in your church where most of your efforts need to be focused in the next 18–24 months?

_____

_____

_____

_____

_____

_____

_____

_____

_____

d. What is the one main thing keeping your church from moving forward at a pace that would be pleasing to God?

_____

_____

_____

_____

2. Plan an evening or weekend retreat devoted to nothing but developing an intentional planning process for your church. This endeavor will be extremely difficult if you attempt to accomplish it during the regularly scheduled meeting times.

3. Schedule a time to objectively analyze and profile the perceptions of your congregation. You cannot move forward until you clearly understand where you are today.

4. Covenant to a clear planning system with steps and stages of accountability.

5. Commit to specific objectives. Agree with your leadership team on 3 to 5 areas of action to which you will devote much of your time and energy as you plan for the future. Assign individuals with leadership skills and a real passion for each area to oversee the planning and implementation process in that area.

4

Goals—Solomon

As the deer panteth for the water,
So my soul longeth after Thee.
You alone are my heart's desire,
And I long to worship Thee.[1]

~·~·~

Obstacles are those frightful things you see when you take your eyes off the goal.

HENRY FORD

~·~·~

Try not. Do or do not. There is no try.

YODA—EMPIRE STRIKES BACK

~·~·~

1. As the Deer. Martin Nystrom. Maranatha Music 1984.

Do you know what the first movie ever made was? Most people don't. Some credit workers in Thomas Edison's lab for making the first film on a continuous strip around 1889–90. Others point to the first movie, *Fred Ott's Sneeze*, copyrighted in 1894 (also by Edison's assistants). Only five seconds long, it's a little short on plot but heavy on action!

Thomas Edison was one of the most brilliant people of his time. He is credited with over 1,000 patents. But Edison was neither content to do all of his work alone nor was he so short-sighted that he failed to develop his inventions even more. He opened factories for making light bulbs and a studio for making films. No one denies that Edison was both smart and practical.

That said, King Solomon is still considered the *wisest* man to have ever lived. There is a difference between wisdom and intelligence. Legends exist of Solomon's wisdom during the visit of the Queen of Sheba, but, in my opinion, the most powerful example of his wisdom is found in the third chapter of First Kings. Two women brought a child to the King—both claiming to be his mother. Rather than listen to the arguing, Solomon ordered a sword to be brought in.

> And the king said, "Bring me a sword." So a sword was brought before the king. And the king said, "Divide the living child in two, and give half to the one and half to the other." 1 Kings 3:24–25

Of course, the real mother stopped the swordsman to save her child's life. King Solomon, using this test to recognize her love, gave her back her son.

As we look at Goals, we are going to look at some aspects from the life of King Solomon. We'll see how he took the vision of his father, King David, and built the Temple. We'll also see how he established goals to complete the objectives required to have a place in which God was honored beyond all other things.

It was an exciting time for the nation of Israel and this should be an exciting time for your church. Keep walking forward as you see what God is doing through you!

Guiding Principle

I'm tired of dreaming. I'm into doing at the moment. It's, like, let's only have goals that we can go after.

BONO (PAUL HEWSON)

~~~

The Challenge of Leadership

The process of setting goals is giving life and straightforward direction to established objectives. As we prayerfully take the next step to seeing God do things through our churches, measurable goals will shed light on our forward path. Visually, we can see footprints in which we are to place our efforts and energies.

To that end, we will consider the following questions:

- How do goals extend our objectives into measurable areas?
- Is there such a thing as a bad goal?
- How many goals are reasonable for each objective?
- How does the church seek God's "success" in setting goals?
- What is the one key element we must never forget in the process?

In this brief chapter, we'll be answering those questions and helping to bring greater definition to a working master plan for your church.

> Brothers, I do not consider that I have made it my own. But one thing I do: forgetting what lies behind and straining forward to what lies ahead, I press on toward the goal for the prize of the upward call of God in Christ Jesus. Philippians 3:13–14

> "But you, take courage! Do not let your hands be weak, for your work shall be rewarded." 2nd Chronicles 15:7

But grow in the grace and knowledge of our Lord and Savior Jesus Christ. To him be glory both now and forever! Amen. 2nd Peter 3:18

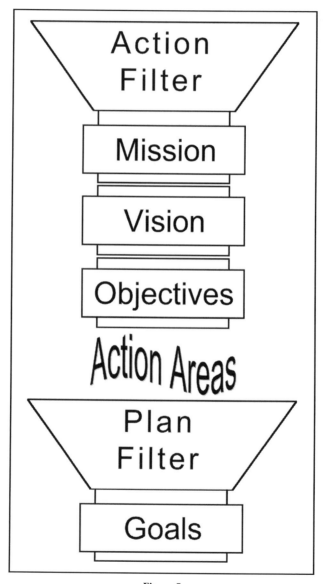

Figure 5

How Do Goals Extend Our Objectives into Measurable Areas?

The reign of King Solomon began with a few problems. He was rushed into the position because someone else wanted the throne and was making steps to take it.

> Now Adonijah the son of Haggith exalted himself, saying, "I will be king." And he prepared for himself chariots and horsemen, and fifty men to run before him. 1st Kings 1:5

For all of the great things shared in Scripture about David's love for the Lord, it would appear that this same passion did not transfer to his children. His eldest, Absalom, had attempted to take the throne (see 2ⁿᵈ Samuel fifteen). Now Adonijah was putting himself forward. However, we see at several points in 1ˢᵗ Kings that Solomon was David's choice. It was not official, but it was known by many.

When Nathan, the prophet, realized what Adonijah was doing, he went to Solomon's mother, Bathsheba. He gave her instructions to save her life, the life of her son and to continue God's plan for Israel. She went to King David and talked to him. He acted.

> And the king swore, saying, "As the Lord lives, who has redeemed my soul out of every adversity, as I swore to you by the Lord, the God of Israel, saying, 'Solomon your son shall reign after me, and he shall sit on my throne in my place,' even so will I do this day." 1 Kings 1:29–30

Solomon was to be the next king. David had sworn that this would be the case. In order for this *objective* to happen, Nathan and Bathsheba acted. They *set goals* to individually see the King, tell him what was happening and wait for his response. Realistically, everything was out of their control. But God blessed their actions and they achieved success.

~~~~

In the process of developing the church's master plan, it is best to proceed systematically while bathing things in prayer. Timelines will be addressed later. For the time being, let's take the previous chapter's objective under evangelism and add a couple of goals. As a reminder, the objective is: *To intentionally increase the opportunities for our members to share their faith with those in their sphere of influence.* (The question of "How?" will be addressed under Strategies.)

Goal-setting is an important step. The acronym "S.M.A.R.T." is often used to differentiate between good and bad goals.

S = Specific—A specific goal is one that is direct and clear to all. Even someone not involved in the process should be able to grasp what you would like to do.

M = Measurable—A measurable goal is one that can be checked for achievement. It should not be answered through a feeling or vague impression.

A = Achievable—While this seems logical, an achievable goal should be one that can definitely be met. In the church, we can set goals that can be met only with God's blessing. Nevertheless, there is a difference between a blessing and an outright miracle! Be bold but do not invite failure through unrealistic expectations.

R = Realistic—A realistic goal is one that is truly desired to be reached. Those pursuing it are willing to take the steps to learn, grow and push towards achievement. There must be the ability to apprehend that knowledge as well!

T = Time-based—A time-based goal has a start date and an end date. While this can be adjusted if needed, the timeline should be clear with evaluation points.

Sample goals for the objective of: *To intentionally increase the opportunities for our members to share their faith with those in their sphere of influence* might include:

1. Each member will complete a three week course on sharing faith.

2. Each member will identify three spheres of influence.

3. Each member will identify two people within each sphere of influence to whom they will prayerfully seek an opportunity to share their faith in the next two months.

4. Each member will seek to invite two people to a fellowship luncheon following Sunday worship on _____.

Using this method, the church leadership can take the bigger objective and begin to focus on concrete and measurable goals. Goals should phrased simply. Further expansion of these goals will occur as Strategies, Timelines and Finances are discussed in subsequent chapters.

Is There Such a Thing as a Bad Goal?

Is there such a thing as a bad goal? Absolutely! Bad goals can cause us to miss our destination completely!

For example, ship captains discovered a troublesome problem in their pursuit of goals. Magnets could cause the compass to deviate from true north. The very thing that should have kept them on course was now getting them lost! They had to find solutions quickly to prevent such deviations.

In the church, we need to keep our eyes open to a goal(s) that would cause us to miss our objective. Again, if we keep our goals short and clear, we can avoid losing direction and focus. A bad goal that lacks clarity and definition must be reworked. Here's a simple test. Ask a teenager (or child) to restate the goals. If they can't, it is not clear enough.

Goals should drive us to complete the objective **God** has given us. If it pushes the agenda of a single person rather than the overall mission and vision of the church, there is a problem.

Not every goal will sound exciting. In fact, a goal like "gathering supplies" might have seemed unexciting to Solomon! But here we caution against a goal that does not provide enough opportunity *to see God at work*. God provided through David a hundred thousand talents of gold. Silver, bronze and other blessings came forward in abundance. A powerful aspect of goals is that they may provide great opportunities to say: "*We can't do this but God can. We need Him to provide XYZ or else this may not proceed.*" Then watch what He does!

How Many Goals are Reasonable?

> In the four hundred and eightieth year after the people of Israel came out of the land of Egypt, in the fourth year of Solomon's reign over Israel, in the month of Ziv, which is the second month, he began to build the house of the Lord. 1 Kings 6:1

A major objective of King Solomon's reign was simple—build a temple. His father David had wanted to build it, but God told him that the honor was to go to his son Solomon. David helped to get some things ready, but the task was in Solomon's hands to complete.

The Temple was to be an incredible testimony to the greatness of God. Cedar, gold, stone, bronze, and pine were used extensively. The interior furnishings were also going to be magnificent. Basins, tables, altars, lamp stands . . . They were all going to be ornate and tremendous demonstrations of the love and glory due to God.

How do you organize the process? GOALS!

It may sound overly simple, but Solomon was able to construct the Temple by carefully setting out goals. Although it isn't laid out as a step-by-step manual in Scripture, the evidence is clear that Solomon proceeded carefully and strategically under God's direction and help from his father David.

With great pains I have provided for the house of the Lord 100,000 talents of gold, a million talents of silver, and bronze and iron beyond weighing, for there is so much of it; timber and stone, too, I have provided. To these you must add. You have an abundance of workmen: stonecutters, masons, carpenters, and all kinds of craftsmen without number, skilled in working gold, silver, bronze, and iron. Arise and work! The Lord be with you!" David also commanded all the leaders of Israel to help Solomon his son . . . 1st Chronicles 22:14–17

Supplies are one thing, but the work still had to be done. Solomon contacted Hiram, king of Tyre for more cedar.

Now therefore command that cedars of Lebanon be cut for me. And my servants will join your servants, and I will pay you for your servants such wages as you set, for you know that there is no one among us who knows how to cut timber like the Sidonians. 1st Kings 5:6

Solomon needed people to do the work as well.

Then Solomon counted all the resident aliens who were in the land of Israel, after the census of them that David his father had taken, and there were found 153,600. Seventy thousand of them he assigned to bear burdens, 80,000 to quarry in the hill country, and 3,600 as overseers to make the people work. 2nd Chronicles 2:17–18

How many goals were set? As few as were required. That should be our intent too!

There is no "magic number" for goals. *The number of goals set should be limited to the number of goals required to accomplish the objective.* Any more will add unnecessary burden to the process. Solomon did not do the work or develop the strategies that were specific to each person. To simplify, Solomon set goals to get the materials, get the workers and get the job moving.

Learn from the man filled with wisdom. *Define the core and keep it simple.*

How Does the Church Seek God's "Success" in Setting Goals?

On his deathbed, King David charged Solomon with great words:

> "I am about to go the way of all the earth. Be strong, and show yourself a man, and keep the charge of the Lord your God, walking in his ways and keeping his statutes, his commandments, his rules, and his testimonies, as it is written in the Law of Moses, that you may prosper in all that you do and wherever you turn, that the Lord may establish his word that he spoke concerning me, saying, 'If your sons pay close attention to their way, to walk before me in faithfulness with all their heart and with all their soul, you shall not lack a man on the throne of Israel.'" 1 Kings 2:2–4

In addition, he recited a few reminders of those he wanted Solomon to deal with (good and bad) after his death. After King David died, Solomon's half-brother Adonijah came with a very disrespectful request and was killed. A priest needed to be removed from service and a former commander was executed. Interestingly, there was one final thing that had to be resolved.

A man named Shimei had called down curses on King David during a difficult time. Rather than killing him, David showed mercy. But he reminded Solomon what had been done before he died. Solomon told Shimei to build a house in Jerusalem and stay there. If he left the city, he would be killed. Shimei agreed. Then, three years later, two of his servants ran away so Shimei went after them. Shimei traveled a fair distance to the city of Gath. When he returned, he was executed. After this, verse forty-six tells us that the *"kingdom was now firmly established in Solomon's hands."*

It's interesting that this was *three years later . . .*

Have you ever noticed that detail? *Three years* passed. Things were still unsettled. How often are we upset if something doesn't happen after only a week? Or a month? Or two months? We want instant gratification.

Patience is a gift. Solomon was blessed—just like his father David—to wait out God's timing. It is through waiting on God that the roots of "success" are strengthened and grow.

Likewise, waiting can help our love grow. Solomon loved God. In worship and sacrifice, he offered a thousand burnt offerings at the altar in Gibeon. God then appeared to him in a dream and asked Solomon what he would like in return for his dedication.

> Solomon said, "You have shown great and steadfast love to your servant David my father, because he walked before you in faithfulness, in righteousness, and in uprightness of heart toward you. And you have kept for him this great and steadfast love and have given him a son to sit on his throne this day. And now, O Lord my God, you have made your servant king in place of David my father, although I am but a little child. I do not know how to go out or come in. And your servant is in the midst of your people whom you have chosen, a great people, too many to be numbered or counted for multitude. Give your servant therefore an understanding mind to govern your people, that I may discern between good and evil, for who is able to govern this your great people?" 1 Kings 3:6–9

God was pleased with this request. Rather than asking for riches or fame, Solomon wanted to be a wise and discerning ruler, led by God. And now we have our model for "success" in setting goals. We must seek God's goals and God's timing.

The process of determining what goals to set to achieve an objective should begin with prayer. Leaders need to set a time to specifically pray for clarity in this part of the process. In the previous chapter, we discussed how important it was for Joshua to put first things first. The Israelites had to be right with God. Likewise, the first requirement in setting goals is for leaders to pray for God's wisdom. They must know what *His* goals are.

We would suggest three specific things to emphasize in the praying process: protection, unity and joy. These three things are found in the prayer of Jesus found in John 17.

> Protection: The word used in verses eleven and fifteen has as one of its roots the idea of a fortress. Jesus did not pray that we would hide behind the walls. Instead, He prayed that we would be guarded while we are part of this world. An image to consider might be one of a tank. Jesus has sent us "out" but prayed that we would be protected when we go. Therefore, as you are praying for God's goals, pray that He would protect you from choosing to do anything outside of His will. If we leave that proverbial tank, we become vulnerable.

> Unity: Over and over again in Scripture, God calls us to unity. Jesus was very clear that we should be one as He and the Father are one. While you may not always agree on everything, pray for unity in going forward. It is possible to act in unity even if there may be some who are unsure.

> Joy: In verse thirteen, Jesus wants us to have a FULL measure of His joy in us. Again, the language emphasizes completeness of this joy. It's not a little happy feeling. It's an exceeding and abundant joy. Pray that God would give you the sense of excitement and expectation that truly overflows.

What is the One Key Element We Must Never Forget in the Process?

How easy is it for us to forget? Forget what? Everything . . .

We forget where we set our keys or our glasses. We forget our computer passwords. We forget birthdays and anniversaries. At times, we even forget why we walked into a room!

But the church must never forget to give glory to God. When you have an opportunity, read the entire chapter of 1st Kings 8 to get the grand picture of the dedication of the Temple. For now, hear the words of praise:

> Then Solomon stood before the altar of the Lord in the presence of all the assembly of Israel and spread out his hands toward heaven, and said, "O Lord, God of Israel, there is no God like you, in heaven above or on earth beneath, keeping covenant and showing steadfast love to your servants who walk before you with all their heart, who have kept with your servant David my father what you declared to him. You spoke with your mouth, and with your hand have fulfilled it this day." 1st Kings 8:22–24

David wanted to build the Temple to honor God. While acknowledging David's desire, God promised him that it would be done through Solomon. In faithfulness, Solomon worked to see this great task completed.

In the beginning of this prayer of dedication, we see Solomon's heart poured out to God. We see his recognition of God's covenant with His people. We see and are reassured that God will continue to be faithful in keeping His promises to us.

And so we praise Him.

Intentionally build into your plans specific times to stop and praise God. Give Him the glory and honor for what He is doing through you. This is a testimony to those around you that all things are being done through His strength and not your own effort.

> [The people] blessed the king and went to their homes joyful and glad of heart for all the goodness that the Lord had shown to David his servant and to Israel his people. 1st Kings 8:66

Action Steps

1. In groups, review the objectives. Set no more than three goals for each objective.

   ### Is it SMART?

   Specific:

   _____

   _____

   _____

   Measurable:

   _____

   _____

   _____

   Achievable:

   _____

   _____

   _____

   Realistic:

   _____

   _____

   _____

Time-Based:

_____

_____

_____

Read John chapter seventeen together. Take some time to gather in prayer. Pray specifically for protection, unity and joy in the days ahead.

5

Strategies—Timothy

When we walk with the Lord in the light of His Word,
What a glory He sheds on our way!
When we do His good will, He abides with us still
And with all who will trust and obey.
Trust and obey, for there's no other way
To be happy in Jesus than to trust and obey.[1]

~,~,~

Before you start anything,
make sure it takes you where you want to go.

ANDY STANLEY

~,~,~

Be vewy vewy quiet, I'm hunting wabbits.

ELMER FUDD

~,~,~

1. *Trust and Obey* text by John H Sammis.

AHOY! IT IS A beautiful day outside. After weeks of anticipation, planning and packing, you are finally ready to embark on the trip of a lifetime—a voyage around the world. The brochure promised you an adventure to remember. You have brought all your supplies aboard the sailboat and are now ready to launch.

But wait . . .

You see a bill of sale on the deck and discover that the captain bought the boat yesterday. As you begin to ask more questions, you discover that his title of captain is questionable. His enthusiasm doesn't change the fact that he has never sailed before. He seems to be afraid of water and then you discover that he can't even swim! And then, the final straw—you catch a glimpse of the book in his pocket—*The Complete Dummy's Guide to Sailing.*

The time to disembark has come . . .

Something was obviously missing in the process. Your objective was clear—to fulfill a lifetime dream of sailing around the world. Your goals were simple—find a company, save the money and pack your bags. Nevertheless, although you were prepared both mentally and physically, one of the strategies was missing. Your goal to find a company did not detail that the captain of the boat had the gifts to do the task. As you look for another way to fulfill your objective, this will certainly be added!

As we delve into setting strategies, we are going to look at someone who was not a neophyte but was definitely facing challenges to his leadership. Timothy was a man identified at a young age (see Acts 16 and 2nd Timothy 1:5) to serve in the early church. He was a student and then a partner in ministry with the Apostle Paul. We see in the letters to Timothy a man who was serving on the front lines. But as we dig deeper, we see a man whom God was using to reach churches throughout the entire region.

Guiding Principle

The typical church in North America is like a sailboat without a rudder, drifting aimlessly in the ocean. As if that is not bad enough, the winds of change and the currents of postmodernism are relentlessly blowing and pulling the church even further off course. I believe that the rudder that the church is missing is a good strategic planning process. Without it, the typical sailor—today's pastor—will find it difficult to navigate in any situation."

AUBREY MALPHURS

~.~.~

The Challenge of Leadership

Strategies give definition to how we will accomplish our goals. While we cannot predict and answer every detail, if we want to fulfill the purpose, vision and objectives God has given, we need to plan and develop strategies to complete the goals through His power and direction.

Leaders in the church are the overseers of the nuts and bolts of the planning process. They must make sure that the strategies that are being developed fall within the bigger picture of God's purpose and vision. Likewise, leaders should work to include the entire body of Christ in the planning and implementation process. Successful plans include as many church members as possible. As the church subscribes to the concept of a faith community in action, its work will have greater impact as they look outside the four walls to see how they are part of Kingdom work.

As we are putting definition to strategies in the church, we will consider the following questions:

- Why does it become so difficult to continue the planning process at this level?

- What is the difference between setting objectives and planning strategy?

- Who is called to serve as a leader as the church moves forward?

- Who should develop the strategies of the church?

- What questions need to be asked in order to develop strategies?

- What are the most common reasons for failure in the goal setting process?

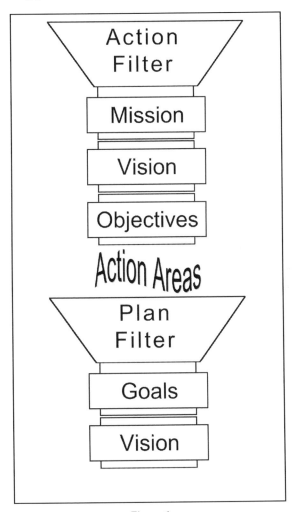

Figure 6

Why does it become so difficult to continue the planning process at this level?

As we first meet Timothy in Acts 16, we learn a few basic facts about him. His mother was a Jewish believer in Jesus. His father was Greek. He was well spoken of by the believers throughout the region. Because he had a Greek father, he had not been circumcised. While this was not a requirement, Paul decided to circumcise him to make ministry a bit easier.

Wait . . .

"make ministry a bit easier"

Does that sound like the Apostle Paul?

If you are familiar with the details around Titus, you see the opposite! Titus was a companion of Paul and a leader for the church in Crete (Titus 1:5). Titus was also a Greek convert. We learned through Galatians that Titus was not circumcised (Galatians 2:3–4). Paul was adamant that circumcision was not a requirement. Let's dig deeper.

There are some interesting differences between the situations. The most notable is that people were trying to *force* Titus to be circumcised. They viewed it as a requirement to salvation. Of course, this was not necessary.

In contrast, Timothy was circumcised simply to make it easier to minister among the Jewish people. There wasn't anything forced. This was not required. It was simply a matter of being expedient. There wouldn't be arguing or questioning. They could move and minister as God led without seeing others stumble.

Think of Paul's powerful words in 1st Corinthians:

> For though I am free from all, I have made myself a servant to all, that I might win more of them. To the Jews I became as a Jew, in order to win Jews. To those under the law I became as one under the law (though not being myself under the law) that I might win those under the law. To those outside the law I became as one outside the law (not being outside the law of God but under the law of Christ) that I might win those outside the law. To the

weak I became weak, that I might win the weak. **I have become all things to all people**, that by all means I might save some. **I do it all for the sake of the gospel**, that I may share with them in its blessings. 1st Corinthians 9: 19–23 (emphasis added)

Paul was concerned about the Gospel. He did not make compromises, but he did act with wise discernment. When appropriate, he adjusted to the situation. He acted according to that which would make it easiest *not* for him to speak. Rather, he acted so that others could *hear*.

And that leads us back to the question: *Why does it become so difficult to continue the planning process at this level?*

The answers can be plentiful. With close to six decades of ministry around the United States and various parts of the world, we have heard a great deal of justification to stop planning. For simplicities sake, we will limit the review to a few snapshot responses—some good and some bad. The first one is actually a Biblical justification.

> We cannot plan God's course. Proverbs 16:9, Jeremiah 10:23 and the often quoted Jeremiah 29:11 scream out that God's Will triumphs. *Amen!* We agree completely. But in making plans, we are not seeking to *contradict* God's will. We are simply seeking to *follow* it. This may require a mental paradigm shift, but viewing the planning process as a time to prayerfully walk His course should conquer our fears and worries and open us to His leading.

> Planning consumes time. Yes, yes it does. But this is not a throwaway time. Taking the time to plan should be seen as an *investment* in the future. Often people will become anxious if the planning has not spurred into action in *their* time frames. Nevertheless, it's not our time. It is God's time.

> Planning may result in failure. Obviously, this is a hard point to contradict. Yes, if we plan and act out that plan, we may fail. But if God is in the plan, should we not step forward in confidence? Fear of failure is not Biblical. If

we do fail, we should not seek to blame. We should seek to learn. What does God want for us?

We need to do—not plan to do. Again, there is great truth in this. But the problem is simple. If we simply all step forward and do whatever we think, we will not be operating in unity and working to walk God's path.

Making plans is a way to make ministry easier. It is a way to proceed forward unified in wisdom and confidence. Paul planned his journeys but listened to God. Timothy learned this very early in the journey with Paul.

> And they went through the region of Phrygia and Galatia, having been forbidden by the Holy Spirit to speak the word in Asia. And when they had come up to Mysia, they attempted to go into Bithynia, but the Spirit of Jesus did not allow them. So, passing by Mysia, they went down to Troas. And a vision appeared to Paul in the night: a man of Macedonia was standing there, urging him and saying, "Come over to Macedonia and help us." And when Paul had seen the vision, immediately we sought to go on into Macedonia, concluding that God had called us to preach the gospel to them. Acts 16:6–10

Wouldn't you rather seek to accomplish God's plan by following God's model?

What Is The Difference Between Setting Objectives And Planning Strategy?

Let's address that question by looking briefly at Paul's missionary journeys. His first journey (Acts 13:4—14:28) departed from Antioch, went to the island of Cyprus and then visited through Galatia before returning. His primary companion was Barnabas.

The second journey (Acts 15:39—18:22) departed from Antioch but took them through Galatia, over to Macedonia, down to Greece, back to Ephesus and ended in Jerusalem. His primary companion was Silas and they were joined by Timothy.

The third journey covered much of the same area but included more cities along the eastern coast of what we now call Turkey. The list of his companions included seven people (Acts 20:4).

But what does that tell us? I think the answer is simple. Paul set objectives, built goals and planned strategies to fulfill those areas of action. How can I state this with certainty?

Let's look at some important contrasts. The first trip was fairly "local" but God blessed it. Miracles happened and many Jews and Gentiles believed. A bit of time passed but Paul and Barnabas then decided to go back and see how these churches and believers were doing. However, in preparing to set out again, Paul and Barnabas had a disagreement. Paul did not want to bring John Mark because of something that had happened in their first journey. Because they disagreed so strongly, they parted company.

In other words, as Paul and Barnabas discussed their *objective* to return to the churches and check on their spiritual life. They set goals of when and how to go. But, in setting those goals, they had a disagreement about their *strategies*. This is worth repeating. They agreed on the *objective* (to meet again with the new disciples) and *goals* (when, where and how to go) but disagreed on the *strategy* (who would be the best members of their team).

Objectives answer the question: *What do we think God is calling us to do?* Goals answer the question: *What steps must we take to achieve the goal?* Strategies answer the question: *How are we going to take those steps?* The intentional plan to get the job done must include clear strategies.

CAUTION: This may feel like it is too much preparation. As some point, you must push off from the dock and start to set sail. While this is absolutely true, over five decades of experience has taught us that preparation is crucial. A carefully laid foundation and a well lit path keeps us focused and directed moving forward in a Strength beyond our own.

> You then, my child, be strengthened by the grace that is in Christ Jesus . . . 2 Timothy 2: 1

Who is Called to Serve as a Leader as the Church Moves Forward?

> Pastoring in the twentieth century requires two things: one, to be a pastor, and two, to run a church. They aren't the same thing.[2]

When I was in my early 20s, I was asked to help drive a moving truck about 3,000 miles—a large portion of which included Mexico, Guatemala and El Salvador. It was an exciting task that I jumped forward to do. Of course, I'd never driven a truck that size or anything for that distance. Why should that stop me? I was willing to serve because I was both honored to be asked and thrilled to have such a challenge.

If only we had the same reactions in the church . . .

Let's look at Timothy some more. He was in a bit of an unusual position. Paul had asked him to stay in Ephesus (1st Timothy 1:3). He gave him authority to refute certain men not to teach false doctrine. Timothy had been with Paul on missionary journeys but this was a both a big change and a big challenge.

Timothy was also evidently not viewed by all in Ephesus as an older, mature leader. Remember, Timothy began his journey with Paul when he was only about 15 years old. Although this was some years later and experience is a great teacher, many people also like to see *physical* maturity. Read through these verses to see that Paul knew some of Timothy's struggles.

> Let no one despise you for your youth, but set the believers an example in speech, in conduct, in love, in faith, in purity. 1st Timothy 4: 12

> No longer drink only water, but use a little wine for the sake of your stomach and your frequent ailments. 1st Timothy 5: 23

> For God gave us a spirit not of fear but of power and love and self-control. 2 Timothy 1:7

2. Eugene Petersen, *Renewing Your Church through Vision and Planning* (Bethany House Publishing 1997)

So, based on these, would you put Timothy in charge of anything?

I would.

Why?

The Apostle Paul was directly called by Jesus Christ to take the message of salvation to the Jews and the Gentiles. He wasn't called by a man—he was called by the Savior. Paul had wisdom and authority. He was actively fulfilling his calling while being led by the Holy Spirit.

In other words, Paul was not someone who would act quickly and foolishly. He moved in prayer while seeking God's wisdom. If Paul appointed Timothy to be a leader to the Ephesians, we should be able to believe that this was God's leading.

And what about the leaders in your church? How is God leading you?

Let's review 1st Timothy 3:

> The saying is trustworthy: If anyone aspires to the office of overseer, he desires a noble task. Therefore an overseer must be above reproach, the husband of one wife, sober-minded, self-controlled, respectable, hospitable, able to teach, not a drunkard, not violent but gentle, not quarrelsome, not a lover of money. He must manage his own household well, with all dignity keeping his children submissive, for if someone does not know how to manage his own household, how will he care for God's church? He must not be a recent convert, or he may become puffed up with conceit and fall into the condemnation of the devil. Moreover, he must be well thought of by outsiders, so that he may not fall into disgrace, into a snare of the devil. 1 Timothy 3:1–7

Do your leaders *desire* to be leaders? Do they move forward in *prayer*? Do they *seek* God's wisdom through the Word?

While many leaders will answer "*Of course!*" we have been in many churches that have a different approach. Key approaches for filling leadership slots tend to be biological. What does that mean? They are looking for warm bodies. Other churches look to the next generation to serve. (*Your grandfather was a leader. Your father was a leader. It's your turn.*) But Paul was clear that a there should be a *desire* to be a leader. There are Biblical qualifications that should *exclude* some people from serving—at least for a season.

This must be clear. If we are approaching the process of setting strategies **Biblically** then we should be sure that our leaders are therefore *Biblically* qualified. The church can affirm the calling through examination but the calling is first and foremost Biblical. While no pastor desires to lose leaders, we must be absolutely convinced that the right people are in the right positions. If God has not called them there, it will be difficult for them, the pastor and the church. This is vital to prayerfully consider before moving forward. Who is called? Those whom *God* is calling!

Who Should Develop The Strategies Of The Church?

The pastor must serve as the *champion* for the mission and vision. The primary vehicle for this is the pulpit. The primary time is Sunday morning. But champions do not limit their activities to an hour or two on one day each week. There must be more times and opportunities to encourage and exhort people to follow God's leading. In addition, the pastor must have people who help and guide in the steps.

While this may again require a bit of a mental paradigm shift for leaders, the issue of "*who does what*" needs to be addressed as we consider who develops strategies. Consider our friend Timothy. He was put in position to guide but he was not going to stay in Ephesus permanently. He had a very key role but his time there was to be brief. Therefore, those who are going to be doing the work need to be a part of determining the work to be done.

It is crucial in this time of strategy development that we expand our circle a bit. In other words, the called leaders have to prayerfully seek God's wisdom in developing the mission, vision, objectives and goals. But as this process proceeds, additional people who oversee key ministry areas are brought into the process.

As we read throughout the Word of God, we see how different responsibilities were given to different people. In 1st Peter 2: 4–10, we read of the priesthood of believers. We have all been called to roles of service. In the church, the professional staff, lay leadership and people in the pews all have roles. Teaching and reaching are shared responsibilities on many, many levels.

God has given your church exactly the leaders and team members that you need to accomplish His purposes. Successful churches are willing to eliminate pride issues and allow the properly gifted leaders and individuals to get the job done.

Present the objectives and goals that will fulfill the mission and vision to the various ministries. Then be honest. Ask the question: *How are we going to get these done?*

Assign key development roles to ministry teams or task forces who will have a part in implementing those strategies. If those people do not have a stake in the plans, ownership, and establishment of check points and accountability, then there will be no responsibility for actually striving to make the strategies come to fruition.

This is one of the most difficult things for a pastor and leadership team to turn over to the lay people. (We can all be guilty of wanting to control things!) However, if the master planning process turns into another list of "things to do" for the pastor and professional staff, the process will be more of a detriment to the church than a benefit.

Truthfully, if those in the church are asked and challenged to step up as leaders, it can add a completely new and exciting passion to the life of the church. God has given your church exactly the leaders and team members that you need to accomplish His purposes. Successful churches are willing to eliminate pride issues and allow the properly gifted leaders and individuals to get the job done. Allow these people to take responsibility for making those strategies work.

This is the difference between having success in following God's plan and killing another tree so a pile of paper can sit in a filing cabinet.

What Questions Need To Be Asked In Order To Develop Strategies?

We have been commissioned to serve the King in spreading the news. We had therefore better be sure that we are doing our very best to serve Him with all that we have.

The goal of the strategy setting process should be to develop a plan that you know you can accomplish with God's help. Successfully accomplishing a God-given challenge encourages us to try again. The blessing of knowing you are a part of God's plan is wonderful!

To be successful, it is necessary to be practical while still fully embracing God's calling to minister. Fred Smith, in his essay, *Secrets to Making Great Decisions*, gives the following list of practical questions to be asked during the decision making process. Keep these in mind as you develop strategies and seek God's blessing.

- *What are our options?*
- *Is this mutually beneficial?*
- *What is the risk?*
- *Is it timely?*
- *Do we have staying power?*
- *What are the long-term ramifications?*
- *Have we built in escape hatches?*
- *Have we asked for advice—after doing our homework?*
- *Have we validated our decisions in prayer?*

Let's take our next step in setting out sample strategies. Remember, the question we must answer in setting strategies is: *How are we going to take those steps?*

Our working objective is: *To intentionally increase the opportunities for our members to share their faith with those in their sphere of influence.* In the previous chapter, we listed four goals. Under each, we will now list strategies:

1. GOAL: Each member will complete a three week course on sharing faith.

    a. A key leader (or the pastor) will find or develop an appropriate curriculum.

    b. Classes will be offered at four different times.

    c. At the conclusion of their class, each member will write their faith story in less than one page.

2. GOAL: Each member will identify three spheres of influence.

    a. Spheres may include family, work, or community.

    b. The spheres should be ones in which they have regular contact.

3. GOAL: Each member will identify two people within each sphere of influence to whom they will prayerfully seek an opportunity to share their faith in the next two months.

    a. The member should begin to pray daily for those individuals.

    b. The identified individuals may be believers or spiritually seeking individuals.

4. GOAL: Each member will seek to invite two people to a fellowship luncheon following Sunday worship on _____.

    a. The church will prepare invitation cards for the members to share.

    b. The purpose of the luncheon will be fellowship and fun in a Christ-centered atmosphere.

Our intent is to strategically develop a clear plan that is bathed in prayer. This plan should generate excitement and enthusiasm for God's people as they anticipate what He will do through them. We now need to move through a discussion of Timelines and Finances. But first, let's answer a simple question.

What Are The Most Common Reasons For Failure In The Strategy Setting Process?

Why did Paul and so many others work so hard to share the message of Jesus Christ with Jews and Gentiles? It's simple. Jesus Christ gave them their mission (Matthew 28: 19–20; Acts 9: 15–16). They were trying to fulfill that mission.

Did they have any failures? One might be able to argue from a human perspective that some of the steps they took were not as successful as others. Being run out of Thessalonica and Berea (Acts 17) were not reasons for patting anyone on the back. The riot in Ephesus (Acts 19) was also not a moment of great joy.

But we can't measure these things in human terms. God is the One in control. We can see how struggles were used to develop a deeper level of faith as they persevered in the difficulties. We are called to persevere! (See Romans 5:3–4; James1: 3–4; 2nd Peter 1: 5–7.) We are called to continue forward so that we can fulfill God's mission.

So why do we so often fail? Leaders generally attribute their *inability* to get things done to one of three areas.

1. *The lack of commitment to take the time to make intentional plans.* If leaders (paid and volunteer) are unwilling to pause from the everydayness of life to make some serious strategic plans for the future, it is no wonder that things will not achieve success. We can be intentional or accidental in ministry (and life). Which would God have you choose?

2. *The unwillingness to organize based on predetermined priorities.* It is incredibly frustrating to actually form a plan

and then have subsequent sabotage (intentional or not) to that plan. Some people do not want anything to change— EVER! There are some individuals who are unwilling to speak up in a group if they disagree. They will then later seek to change or implement the opinions that were not expressed. This will result in difficulties and failure.

3. *The lack of discipline to act on the plans developed.* To have the privilege of working in the church is truly an incredible gift (even if it doesn't feel like it all the time). A volunteer labor force is also an incredible gift. However, if volunteers (or paid staff) are unwilling to move forward because of other priorities, action is necessitated by the leadership. Staff must be corrected. Volunteers must be encouraged and taught the value of their labor of service to the King. Discipline in labor is honoring Him.

If we believe that we have been called by God to fulfill His purposes, then we must not let the things (or people) of this world stop us. We must press on and persevere.

> Not that I have already obtained all this, or have already been made perfect, but I press on to take hold of that for which Christ Jesus took hold of me. Brothers, I do not consider myself yet to have taken hold of it. But one thing I do: Forgetting what is behind and straining toward what is ahead, I press on toward the goal to win the prize for which God has called me heavenward in Christ Jesus. Philippians 3:12–14

Action Steps

1. Evaluate your emotional condition and analyze your passion as a leader in the church. Make sure that you are involved with ministry that truly corresponds to your passion. If not, changes need to be made. God-determined ministry should be joyful.

2. Consider the following areas. Rank from one (highest) to seven (lowest) where you spend your time. Estimate the number of hours spent in an average week (excluding sleep).

ACTIVITY	RANK	%TIME SPENT
Occupation	_____	_____
Family	_____	_____
Leisure Activities	_____	_____
Church Work	_____	_____
Personal Time	_____	_____
Community Activities	_____	_____
Other	_____	_____

> Spend a few moments in prayer reflecting on this list. Are there areas in which God would be better served if you shifted priorities or some time? Consider some personal strategies to change or strengthen those activities in the next twelve months.

3. Inventory Spiritual Gifts. As a leader, are you using your gifts properly? Do you have someone in your church that is helping individual members to find and use their gifts to the service of the King? Who is / should that person be?

4. Celebrate blessings! Publish the objectives, strategies and timelines. After successfully seeing God bring an objective to completion through His people or after meeting a key timeline of a strategy, publish that information. Nothing is

more refreshing, encouraging and satisfying than actually doing the things that you have set out to do as a body. Confidence will also be built and future successes assured as you accomplish more and more of your objectives.

5. PRAY! Reinforce prayer and seeking glory to the King as you continue to develop and implement strategies

6

Timelines and Finances—Esther

Little is much when God is in it,
Labor not for wealth or fame;
There's a crown and you can win it,
If you go in Jesus' name.[1]

A bucket with a hole in the bottom gets just as empty
as one kicked over.

ANONYMOUS

Darlin', forever is a long long time.
And time has a way of changin' things.

BIG MAMA (FOX AND THE HOUND)

---

1. *Little is Much When God is in it* text by Kittie L Suffield.

A CHALLENGE FOR EVERY young person is to run the mile in school. I have had a chance to watch a couple of classes go through this process. As odd as this may sound, it can be fascinating to watch the different types of runners.

Sprinters explode off the line with a fury, but, as the run progresses, they begin to slow down and feel the results of the distance. Some choose to walk the distance without trying. Wise runners set a pace from the start. Realizing it is a journey, they find a pace that will allow them to complete the task in a reasonable time without overtaxing themselves. As they pass the sprinters (now the walkers!), the probability of success will encourage them to continue.

What does this have to do with planning? Planning is a *process*, not a race.

The journey will never be completed if the tasks are rushed. We must be able to give the proper balance of patience and faith development to planning. Patience is crucial because we may not all be at the same point in wanting to see the church move forward. Some of the small, planned changes that need to be implemented will take time to allow for people to process the need for and concepts behind such steps.

Conversely, we cannot have an unreasonably slow attitude modeled. If we keep delaying important steps, then those who are ready will become frustrated. While it is important to allow God to mold and shape hearts, it will be detrimental to the long term goals if the attitude is consistently *wait, wait, wait . . .*

Time is actually a very helpful tool in the conceptual framework of time. As timelines are set, plans take on an element of reality. Timelines establish targets that in turn demand accountability. If we say that we are going to accomplish something by a certain date, then on that date, we will have to take an inventory to see if we got the job done.

In a volunteer environment, this can be a frightening concept. When effort is called for without the benefit of compensation, it can be very challenging to check on progress. Individuals can resent questions even though they come with good intentions. Nevertheless, in order to be successful, timelines must be in place. Leaders in the church can help overcome the hurdle of fear by modeling their own efforts. By publishing objectives, strategies AND the timelines, others will see the work being attempted and the results. Honesty is crucial as is the celebration of success. Although this should never be done for pride or glory, if completed tasks are lauded in private and public, enthusiasm can be generated for moving ahead.

As we consider these two important parts of the process, we are going to take a quick look at the life of Esther. This Old Testament queen served an important role in the protection of God's people as they faced a harsh enemy determined to erase the Jewish people from the land. We can learn a lot from this woman who agreed to step forward in faith—even if death was the result.

Guiding Principle

Further, take heed that you faithfully perform the business you have to do in the world, from a regard to the commands of God; and not from an ambitious desire of being esteemed better than others.

DAVID BRAINERD

The Challenge of Leadership

In this section, we will discuss both timelines and finances. Although these are small areas, it is important that leaders understand and plan through these practical aspects with a clear and consistent Biblical approach.

A vital aspect of these two areas is communication. There must be internal communication among staff. There must be communication among the pastoral and lay leadership. There must be communication to the church family at large. Each of these circles of communication must have clear and direct information from those who are intimately involved in the process. Ownership is an aspect that all in the church should have for the carrying out of God's mission.

As we are putting timelines and finances in the church, we will consider the following questions:

- What are timelines and how do they demonstrate faith?

- What is the role of checkpoints in timelines?

- How can we best establish measureable timelines?

- What are some financial considerations that need to be identified?

- How will we communicate these to the church family?

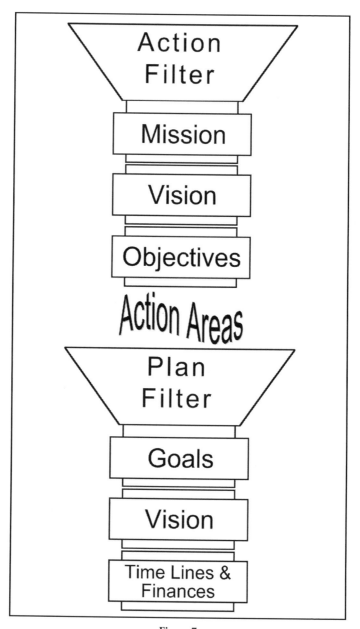

Figure 7

What are Timelines
and How Do They Demonstrate Faith?

As we are introduced to the characters in Esther, it can be helpful to gather a bit of understanding of the setting. The story begins in the citadel of Susa (1:2). King Xerxes hosts a great feast and, during the feast, orders Queen Vashti to present herself and display her beauty. There is a great deal of speculation about some special circumstances regarding how she was to step out, but she refused her drunken husband. Because of this perceived act of disrespect, she was banished from the king's presence and he sought a new queen.

The process of finding a queen was not simple. Beautiful girls from throughout the area were brought to the palace. There were rituals that included months of beauty treatments and special food. The king would then pick from among the women to choose the next queen. As we know, a young lady by the name of Esther was chosen.

Esther was Jewish. She had lost her parents and been raised by her uncle, Mordecai. He had forbidden her to reveal her nationality (2:10). We are not exactly sure why but it is very possible there was some anti-Jewish sentiment.

What does this have to do with timelines?

The book of Esther presents *two* versions of timelines: accidental and intentional. The situation surrounding Vashti's fall and Esther's rise would be seen through human eyes as accidental (or circumstantial). It was not planned by Xerxes, Mordecai or anyone else involved. It had great purpose in God's plan, but it would appear to be circumstantial to those involved.

In the church, we can likewise have many things that *appear* to be happening by accident. Someone dies suddenly. A new family arrives or a long-time family leaves. We aren't sure why or what is happening but there is an air of uncertainty about the future as a result. We forget God's sovereignty as we push forward.

Alternatively, we can have things happen *intentionally*. Let's explore.

A man named Haman was deeply against Mordecai. Mordecai refused to kneel down and pay Haman any honor. As a result, Haman plotted to kill all of the Jewish people. (He did not know Esther was Jewish.)

When Mordecai learned of this plot, he went to Esther and encouraged her to go before King Xerxes and try to save her people. Unfortunately, she could not approach the king without his permission or risk the penalty of death. Nevertheless, Mordecai counseled her to do it anyway:

> For if you keep silent at this time, relief and deliverance will rise for the Jews from another place, but you and your father's house will perish. And who knows whether you have not come to the kingdom for such a time as this? Esther 4: 14

Esther agreed. She asked for prayer by the Jewish people but she was willing to put her life on the line. She then put on her royal robes and took a chance. She was granted favor but she didn't jump right in to the full request. She invited the king—and the evil Haman—to a banquet. They attended and the king offered her up to half the kingdom. (What a banquet it must have been!)

Instead of receiving it, she asked that they attend another banquet.

What a strange request . . .

But they agreed . . .

Later, Haman boasted to his family and friends about the banquet and how important he thought he was. However, rather than being content and focusing on the joy and blessing, he also shared his displeasure that Mordecai was still alive. Why was he so upset? Mordecai was scheduled for death so this impatience was odd . . .

As an answer to this frustration, Haman had a gallows built so Mordecai could be hanged *immediately*. Before this could be done, in a perfectly God-designed twist, Xerxes had Haman parade Mordecai through the city in honor! (Esther 5:14—6:11)

This was not what Haman expected. His wife and advisors later told him that this was not going to end well. They could see there was a God who was moving things outside of Haman's desires.

When the second banquet was held, Esther revealed that she was Jewish. And again, God has a twist in mind as Haman was hung on the newly-built gallows. Xerxes authorized Mordecai to issue a decree that allowed the Jewish people to arm and defend themselves. The Jewish people were saved!

How was this intentional?

Circumstances developed and put the Jewish people in a situation outside of their control. Mordecai acted by communicating with Esther. [God's sovereignty was still acknowledged (4:14).] The Jewish people acted by praying and fasting. Esther acted by going to the king.

Each step was an intentional act to do everything they could do when things seemed so out of control. They acted quickly and decisively. They had a very clear timeline because the threat of genocide was imminent.

Now, let's get personal. *How do you feel about your church?*

Our culture now changes at an incredibly fast rate. Any example listed would be out of date by the time this book is published. iPhones, iPads, "i" everything . . . Things that were unheard of only a decade ago are now the norm.

We establish timelines because we are seeking to do everything we can to intentionally follow God's plan. We recognize that He is ultimately in control as we step forward in faith and prayer. We need to pray, seek God's will and decisively set clear timelines.

What are the Roles of Checkpoints in Timelines?

While driving down from the summit of Pike's Peak in Colorado, you are required to stop at a checkpoint. At this checkpoint, they record the temperature of your brakes. Why? They learned the hard way that many people ride their brakes and brakes may fail when they get too hot. If your brakes are unsafe at the checkpoint, you have to wait while they cool off.

Checkpoints are defined as points at which we evaluate progress. They help us make sure we are doing what needs to be done and do not get off course. For example, the Jewish people had a real date (9:1–5) for which they had to prepare—the thirteenth day of the twelfth month. They needed to prepare and plan for this pending attack with every minute BEFORE the date arrived. Likewise, a date will give us clarity and a sense of definitive purpose on which we can focus our efforts.

Checkpoints are therefore vital for gauging the real actions. They put dates on the calendar and help make the goals real. There is nothing like seeing that target date for completion and knowing what we have to get done along the way. Each checkpoint is a part of the process to reaching the goal. And yes, procrastination is always possible. However, it is NOT desirable. The best thing to do is set a timeline with concrete checkpoints and stick to them.

How Can We Best Establish Measurable Timelines?

Let's first define the word "measurable." If something is capable of being measured, that means we can gauge the capacity or boundaries of that particular object. For a *timeline* to be measurable, we must be able to determine whether or not the completion of the task is accomplishable within the boundaries of time that are available. In simple words, can we get it done in the time we have?

Time is fixed. What does this mean? I always bake my wife a cake for her birthday. Unfortunately, I'm not always the best in preparing for the project. Even when I think I'm doing ok, I don't always give myself enough time to accomplish the task. To prepare a birthday cake—icing and all—you need a minimum of two hours. There must be time to prepare the batter, bake, cool and frost. While there are a few tricks that can shave a minute or two, those are incredibly minor. (I've learned you can put a cake in the freezer to help it cool faster!)

Therefore, our best course of action is to "*Begin with the end in mind.*" When does the effort need to be completed? Work back from that point.

- What are the key components? What do we have to do?

- At what point should those components be completed? What is the latest date / time?

- Can components be done at the same time or are they interdependent? In other words, is there something that must be done first in order for the next action to be accomplished?

- How can we check those components? If there are several people involved, have we put in place opportunities and means for communication?

- Are the components within the timelines really measurable?

- What do we do if they are not completed? Do we have a back-up plan?

This may seem like a lot of work, but the more planning done on the front end, the better. These insure action and allow leaders to obtain reports on progress without seeming to put undue pressure on the individuals serving in the various ministries.

What are Some Financial Considerations that Need to be Identified?

In Luke 14, Jesus is speaking to the crowds about the cost of becoming a disciple. He uses an illustration of a man building a tower.

> For which of you, desiring to build a tower, does not first sit down and count the cost, whether he has enough to complete it? Otherwise, when he has laid a foundation and is not able to finish, all who see it begin to mock him, saying, "This man began to build and was not able to finish." Luke 14: 28–30

Many churches have unfortunately set out with a vision but neglected to sufficiently count the cost. A persuasive leader will put out a bold challenge and people respond—for a season. Unfortunately, if something happens and that momentum is halted, it can take a great effort to reinitiate life. This can be tragic.

Several years ago, I watched as a church prepared to make a very radical move. The leaders felt they needed to close their current location and move to a more affluent community. While it was a bold vision, within a year, the senior pastor left, leadership fell apart and the church defaulted on its loan. They felt as if they were moving in the right direction but, in clear hindsight, they could see how they failed to count the complete cost. Not only was this hurtful to the church family, it gave a poor witness to those in the surrounding community.

Here are some questions to ask:

1. Should this be supported as a budgeted line item?

2. Should this be supported via a special fund?

3. Should this be supported via special fundraisers?

4. What will happen if sufficient funds are not contributed?

5. What will supporting this endeavor do to the rest of the budget?

6. What will happen if the allocated funds for this project stop being available?

7. What will happen if there are designated funds in excess of the budget?

These are seven short questions that should be prayerfully considered before moving forward. Ask your leaders if they have any more. Be clear and up front about concerns that may exist. If God provides the resources for the project, praise His Name and give Him all the glory.

Continuing the Example

In the previous sections, we have been using the working objective of: *To intentionally increase the opportunities for our members to share their faith with those in their sphere of influence.*

As we have expanded this objective to include goals and strategies, let us now add timelines and finances.

1. GOAL: Each member will complete a three week course on sharing faith.

   a. A key leader (or the pastor) will find an appropriate curriculum.

      i. The curriculum will be presented for approval at the next leadership meeting.

      ii. The cost of the curriculum will be covered in the church budget.

   b. Classes will be offered at four different times.

      i. One class will be offered on Sunday mornings.

      ii. One class will be offered in the evenings.

      iii. Childcare will be provided for one class.

   c. At the conclusion of their class, each member will write their faith story in less than one page.

      i. The faith story will be shared with the class the following week.

      ii. Faith stories will not be edited but suggestions can be made to keep clear and brief. Listeners should seek to encourage!

2. GOAL: Each member will identify three spheres of influence.

   a. Spheres may include family, work, or community.

   b. The spheres should be ones in which they have regular contact.

3.   GOAL: Each member will identify two people within each sphere of influence to whom they will prayerfully seek an opportunity to share their faith in the next two months.

    a.   The member should begin to pray daily for those individuals.

    b.   The identified individuals may be believers or spiritually seeking individuals.

        i.   Members should be willing to commit personal resources if appropriate for buying a lunch or cup of coffee.

4.   GOAL: Each member will seek to invite two people to a fellowship luncheon following Sunday worship on _____

    a.   The church will prepare invitation cards for the members to share.

        i.   All printing will be done by the church.

        ii.   Invitation cards will be distributed one month prior to the lunch.

    b.   The purpose of the luncheon will be fellowship and fun in a Christ-centered atmosphere.

        i.   The church will cover the cost of the meal so that members can focus on their invited guests. (If possible, find a partner church that is willing to help with serving. Then reciprocate!)

        ii.   There will be no speaker for the lunch but a mix of appropriate Christian music will be played in the background.

        iii.   Tracts and / or other resources will be purchased by the church and available for anyone who wishes.

Please understand that these are NOT the only ways in which you may wish to proceed. These are suggestions only. Each church must determine what is appropriate for their own family. For example, one church may have great impacts through fellowship lunches while another may find it beneficial to have a special speaker or musician. (This is another illustration of the focus versus form issue.)

The intent is to be effective in presenting the love and light of Jesus Christ. As people see Him through the members of the church, visitors will begin to ask questions and may be led into a personal relationship with Him. God changes the heart. We are called to reflect Him.

How Will This be Communicated to the Entire Church Family?

Have you noticed that people seem to care a great deal about time and money? And yet, even when we wish we had more time to study, we but still manage to sit and watch hours of TV. When we wish we could put more money into savings, we still manage to afford to eat out. When challenged about this dichotomy, we justify our actions.

There is one crucial thing to remember before discussing the communication principles. Financial expert Dave Ramsey shares that there are over 800 references to money in Scripture. Why? The simple answer is that God knows how tightly we hold onto money. It would seem to be the one thing that we hold onto most tightly. If there is a perception that this is all about money, people will be less likely to become a part of the process. Be clear that you are seeking to carry out what you believe is God's plan!

As we prayerfully develop God's plan for our church, we need to keep communication active and alive. The more we keep people involved and engaged through regular and inspirational updates, the more investment they will have in the overall process. Then, when we are ready to launch key components, they will be more excited to be a part of it all.

Let's boil down communication to three key elements: the sender, the receiver and the delivery system.

> The Sender: The sender should be able to speak to the issue in an appropriate manner that will communicate the importance of the message. There is great value in varying the sender. If the same person reads the announcements or if the same method is used every time, the receiver learns to disconnect.

> The Receiver: We need to give consideration the target audience. How will younger audiences "hear" announcements versus the methods through which an older audience will receive something? For example, oftentimes a teenager will read a text message or Facebook page before they answer a phone.

> The Delivery System: It is also beneficial to vary the delivery system. The importance of the communication should give weight to how that is to be shared. Simple updates can be shared in writing. Something that is more time sensitive or crucial to the long term project should be shared verbally. In addition, the greater the importance of a message, the more unique or the smaller the group should be. If something is vital, we need to make sure that people truly hear it! The same written announcement in a bulletin for three weeks will decrease the response rate. Communication and marketing professionals typically suggest that you plan to share each message three times in three different ways.

To be clear, that is not just one time.

It is not two times.

It is three times.

Much, much, much more could be said about communication. For the best communication in the future, we should remember to do three things: Evaluate, Adjust and Communicate. Evaluate how the message was sent and received. Make adjustments to improve future communications. And communicate again, and again, and again.

> Our biggest communication failure is a failure to communicate . . .

Action Steps

1. Discuss the concept of timelines. Are the leaders willing to hold one another accountable to following a schedule? How can this best be done in an encouraging manner? What are realistic and measurable checkpoints for the process?

2. Consider a visual that might help with keeping leaders and members of the church engaged with the process. For example, can there be a posted chart showing progress points? Would it help to have a "Three-month list," a "Six-month list," a "One-year list" and a "Three-year list" to illustrate things that are on the immediate or the longer-term horizons? Use something that works for your church and encourage people when God blesses in a step!

3. Financial discussions are a difficult aspect of ministry. While we must be good stewards, we must also be willing to take steps of faith. Discuss the seven questions presented in the financial considerations section. How comfortable are the leaders when answering these? Are there any to add?

4. Communication and evaluation are keys to moving forward. Consider the following areas and evaluate them in relationship to current church systems.

COMMUNICATION	EFFECTIVENESS	IMPROVEMENTS
Announcements		
Bulletin		
Newsletter		

Web Site _____   _____

Email Database _____   _____

Other _____   _____

Other _____   _____

Other _____   _____

As you prayerfully reflect on the list above, don't forget to consider how you might change things up a bit. Would it be beneficial to have announcements at a different time? Does the web site need a facelift? Can you ask someone from the outside to review any of these areas to offer a different perspective?

5. PRAY! Do not forget that you are serving the King! You don't know what God can do through the leaders He has called to serve the church at this time!

PART THREE

Doing the Work

7

Implementation—Peter

Lead on, O King Eternal, We follow, not with fears;
For gladness breaks like morning, Where'er Thy face appears.
Thy cross is lifted o'er us; We journey in its light.
The crown awaits the conquest; Lead on, O God of might.[1]

Genius is one percent inspiration
and ninety-nine percent perspiration.

THOMAS ALVA EDISON

There is no greater burden than great potential.

LINUS VAN PELT (*PEANUTS* BY CHARLES M. SCHULZ)

1. *Lead On, O King Eternal* text by Ernest W. Shurtleff.

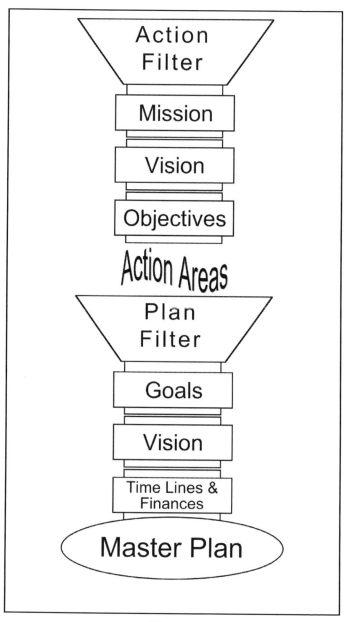

Figure 8

IMAGINE STEPPING UP TO the plate in the seventh game of the World Series at the bottom of the ninth inning. There are two outs and no one is on base. The score is tied. Everything rests on your shoulders because in the last inning your last pitcher was hit by a ball and broke his thumb. If you can't get on base, the game is essentially over.

As you dig in, you suddenly realize you don't have a bat in your hands! You turn to call time out, but the pitcher—realizing your colossal blunder—has already started the pitch. However, in his haste, the pitch actually hits you on the arm. You shake it off and head to first. After you take a small two-step lead, the pitcher inexplicably throws over to first. His anger at his previous mistake is increased as the ball evades the first baseman. You sprint to second.

The first baseman heaves the ball well over the head of the second baseman and you proceed to third. The outfielder that has come in to back up the second baseman trips over the ball and it rolls into the corner. You have unbelievably managed to score the winning run without ever touching a bat!

Is it possible? Yes it is. Is it probable? Certainly not. Years of training and study would prevent experienced professionals from making such an obvious mistake. The three compounded errors by other professionals make such a scenario ludicrous.

And yet . . .

At moments of weakness, is it possible that even the greatest among us will make a mistake. We want to do great things. We feel challenged to do great things. We believe we are empowered to do great things.

And yet . . .

> Simon Peter said to him, "Lord, where are you going?" Jesus answered him, "Where I am going you cannot follow me now, but you will follow afterward." Peter said to him, "Lord, why can I not follow you now? I will lay down my life for you." Jesus answered, "Will you lay down your life for me? Truly, truly, I say to you, the rooster will not crow till you have denied me three times." John 13: 36–38

> The servant girl at the door said to Peter, "You also are not one of this man's disciples, are you?" He said, "I am not." John 18:17
> Now Simon Peter was standing and warming himself. So they said to him, "You also are not one of his disciples, are you?" He denied it and said, "I am not." One of the servants of the high priest, a relative of the man whose ear Peter had cut off, asked, "Did I not see you in the garden with him?" Peter again denied it, and at once a rooster crowed. John 18:25-27

Peter was the most confident, brash and aggressive of the disciples. Typically the first to speak and act, Peter was vulnerable to the results of his hasty actions. (Stepping out of boats fully clothed was one of the most interesting examples!) This behavior and impulsiveness eventually resulted in a temporary separation from the other disciples (Mark 16: 7) and a beautiful scene of restoration with the resurrected Christ (John 21: 15-17). Regardless of the situation, this disciple was almost always ready to go into action.

Does God expect us to really work?

> In the beginning . . . Genesis 2: 2: *The LORD God took the man and put him in the Garden of Eden to work it and keep it.*
> In Jesus' ministry . . . Luke 10: 1-2: After this the Lord appointed seventy-two others and sent them on ahead of him, two by two, into every town and place where he himself was about to go. And he said to them, "The harvest is plentiful, but the laborers are few. Therefore pray earnestly to the Lord of the harvest to send out laborers into his harvest."
> In the early church . . . Ephesians 2: 8-10: For by grace you have been saved through faith. And this is not your own doing; it is the gift of God, not a result of works, so that no one may boast. For we are his workmanship, created in Christ Jesus for good works, which God prepared beforehand, that we should walk in them.

Peter exemplifies the type of attitude Christians *need* to have towards work. Granted we must be a little more patient, but we should be aggressively seeking opportunities to put faith into action. As we look at Peter's life and letters, we see his maturation from leap first—look second—to a seasoned, dedicated disciple. The value of planning and moving with God became his method of operation. We pray. We plan. We act.

Scripture is clear that God created us with a purpose in mind. We must be ever-seeking His will and His strength to accomplish that purpose.

This is our calling as Christians.

This is the work of the Church.

Guiding Principle

When I stand before God at the end of my life, I would hope that I would not have a single bit of talent left, and could say, "I used everything you gave me."

ERMA BOMBECK

The Challenge of Leadership

Although she is not noted as a theologian, Erma Bombeck shared some deeply motivating words that serve as a challenge for Implementation. This is the final area in our design of developing and carrying out God's Master Plan for our church. No matter what has gone on before and how productive our planning, it is all for nothing if we fail to implement those plans. Leaders must be the drivers that make it happen.

The Master Planning process is just that—a process. It is one that must be strategic and thoughtful. But it must be created and carried out in an environment of prayer and searching the Word. This "atmosphere" is developed by leaders setting the tone and example. As has been said, *a stream will not rise higher than its source*. If leaders do not model, people will not follow.

There are still a few difficult questions that need to be addressed in light of the work that is required to lead an effective church. As we discuss these questions, we will look at issues of action, evaluation, accountability, refinement, and communication. This may seem like a lot to consider, but these are vital for healthy implementation.

- Once a plan is in place, why is it crucial that we persevere?

- Why do we need to set up systems for evaluation?

- What about accountability? Is it a Scriptural phenomenon?

- When do we make adjustments to the plan?

- How do we keep the process of master planning alive?

- What will be our greatest barrier to success?

Our example is the Apostle Peter. How did he lead in carrying out the commission given to him by Jesus Christ? How did he work with others? It's a fascinating study to embrace and carry forward to see God's plan bear fruit in His church!

> Show me your faith apart from your works, and I will show you my faith by my works. James 2: 18b

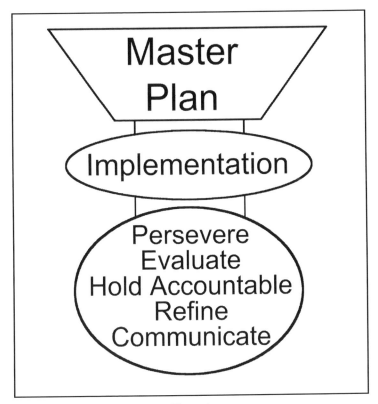

Figure 9

Once The Plan Is In Place, Why Is It Crucial That We Persevere?

Bad leaders fail.
Great leaders fail.
Bad and great leaders fail.
But the difference is that great leaders don't let failures stop them. Great leaders learn from failure.

"Many of life's failures are people who did not realize how close they were to success when they gave up." Thomas Edison

True leaders don't view failure as an end. True leaders view failures as a step in the journey to achieving the results they believe they are called to achieve. While there are examples from Peter's life, as we consider this challenge to persevere, we are going to look at an example from the early church and the Apostle Paul.

In his second letter to the church in Thessalonica, Paul shared with them that he boasted about their perseverance.

> Therefore we ourselves boast about you in the churches of God for your steadfastness and faith in all your persecutions and in the afflictions that you are enduring. 2 Thessalonians 1:4

Of course, we need to know through what they were persevering. What sort of persecution and trials were they enduring? For the answer, let's look at Acts 17.

> Now when they had passed through Amphipolis and Apollonia, they came to Thessalonica, where there was a synagogue of the Jews. And Paul went in, as was his custom, and on three Sabbath days he reasoned with them from the Scriptures, explaining and proving that it was necessary for the Christ to suffer and to rise from the dead, and saying, "This Jesus, whom I proclaim to you, is the Christ." And some of them were persuaded and joined Paul and Silas, as did a great many of the devout Greeks and not a few of the leading women. But the Jews were jealous, and taking some wicked men of the rabble, they formed a mob, set the city in an uproar, and attacked the house of Jason, seeking to bring them out to the crowd. Acts 17: 1–5

In the ninth chapter of Acts, Paul (Saul) was literally knocked off his horse and called by Jesus Christ. Although the physical aspects of the calling were different, it was the same calling as Peter received. They were both called to carry the message of the Gospel to all nations. But, while Peter's apostolic ministry was concentrated heavily in the Judea and Samaria area (going as far to the north as Caesarea Maritima), Paul was set apart (Acts 13: 2–3) for a special mission ministry.

When Paul arrived in a town, he went to the synagogue. It was to this audience that he first shared the message of the Messiah. But Paul did not stop with the Jewish people. He would also share the message with the Gentiles. As we can see in the Acts seventeen account, this would make the Jewish people rather upset. Riots and mobs tended to follow Paul's ministry as a result.

If you continue reading the account, we see where Paul was sent away at night to Berea for his protection. But the Jewish people from Thessalonica followed him. They were determined to stop Paul. Paul was sent away yet again to another town.

The point is this: *The Jewish leaders in Thessalonica wanted to stop people from believing in Jesus as the Messiah.* The first letter Paul wrote stated that they received the message in "great affliction." Even so, their faith had become known throughout the region. They faced strong opposition and false teachers but they were standing strong.

They were persevering.

The point is this. If we look at Paul's steps into Thessalonica from one point of view, we could say that he failed. He was chased out of town in the dark of night. Those who gave him shelter were taken prisoner and forced to pay fines. It would not have been encouraging.

But we have to look at *what God did.*

God called people to faith and they responded. Things were not perfect, but they acted in faith, stood strong and persevered. Their story became known throughout the region. Their story is known **today** in churches around the world.

We do not know what God will do through your leaders and your church. It is possible that the impact of your actions today may not be known for a generation or more. That's in God's hands. For today, we persevere in the storms and trials that may come about because we know *Who* holds the future!

Why Do We Need To Set Up Systems For Evaluation?

As we read Doctor Luke's account in the book of Acts, we see God doing incredible things in the early church. People were even bringing their sick into the streets and putting them on mats so that Peter's shadow might pass over some of them (Acts 5:15). This may seem extreme, but people recognized the great things that God was doing through the Apostles.

Instead of reacting with rejoicing, the high priest and the Sadducees had much the same response as they did to the ministry of Jesus Christ. They began to persecute the believers and threw them into prison. That night, an angel appeared, opened the doors and let them out. The apostles were given instructions to continue telling the people the full message of the Gospel.

It's interesting to see what happens next. When the high priest called together the Sanhedrin (the full assembly of the elders of the Jewish church), they sent for their prisoners. However, their prisoners were no longer in prison! The cell doors were locked and the guards were still in place but the cells were empty.

Imagine the shock when someone noticed the apostles teaching the people in the Temple Courts! Once again, Peter and the other Apostles defied *human* logic by following the commands of God.

And that is the principle for each one of us to remember as we consider the systems for evaluation. The plans we seek to make are not *our* plans. We should have no ownership of them other than to have been the hands that held the pen and are following those instructions.

> *Evaluation is required so that we are confident we are staying on the path.*

What will this confidence bring us? As we continue reading the narrative in Acts, we see that the Apostles were "excused" for a moment. The famous Pharisee and teacher, Gamaliel, instructed them to proceed carefully. They were to consider what had happened during two past events. Two men had led some others astray. After they died, their followers fell away. It proved that those efforts were of human origin. If this radical sect (as they were considered) was also simply as movement of the day, it would fall away. Gamaliel advised:

> So in the present case I tell you, keep away from these men and let them alone, for if this plan or this undertaking is of man, it will fail; but if it is of God, you will not be able to overthrow them. You might even be found opposing God!" So they took his advice . . . Acts 5:38–39

Over two thousand years later, men and women are still giving their lives for the Truth of the Good News of Jesus Christ. *Gamaliel gave wise advice . . .*

What About Accountability? Is It A Scriptural Phenomenon?

The church is an unusual organism. The *"priesthood of believers"* or the *"saints called by God to accomplish His ministry"* do much of the work. Serving in the church is a very lofty calling. However, (using secular terms) if we consider the bulk of our workforce, that workforce translates into volunteers. Volunteers may have great hearts but sometimes lack full commitment.

Most people *want* to do their assigned tasks well. They *want* to serve the Lord. However, given the opportunity to postpone or avoid the accomplishment of their ministry tasks, they often will. This is the unfortunate result of the sinful nature.

Leaders MUST set up systems to check that God's goals are being accomplished. In the early implementation stages of the plan, the establishment of precedence is very important. Most workers will take their lead as to whether the process is serious or not based on early reactions to work completed or not completed.

Leaders must lovingly exhort those who are falling behind and enthusiastically applaud those who are working according to the plan. All must understand that the work that is being done

Giving Life to Vision

is important, significant and essential to the accomplishment of the master plan.

Accountability is a natural step of the process of implementation.

Peter was called by Jesus Christ to serve as a leader in the Church. However, even Peter was not free to act without accountability. Let's go back to Acts and spend a moment looking at an example of Peter being brought before other church leaders with some strong criticism.

In Acts chapter 10, we read of a man named Cornelius. He was a Roman centurion—a very powerful man who was "devout and God-fearing." (In other words, he wasn't Jewish but he was a follower of the teachings of Judaism.) Cornelius had a vision to send for Peter.

Peter likewise had a vision. However, this vision involved the eating of animals that Jewish dietary law considered unclean. Peter would not violate that law but he was commanded in the dream to not call anything impure that God considered clean. Peter was trying to figure out this vision when he was commanded by the Spirit to go with men to the house of Cornelius.

Then God moved . . .

Peter shared and the Holy Spirit filled the household of Cornelius. They were all baptized in the Name of Jesus Christ. It was an incredible time of praise and joy!

Then people reacted . . .

Peter went back to Jerusalem and had to "answer" for what he had done (Acts 11). "Circumcised" believers (meaning they were in outward agreement with the Law) did not agree with Peter going into the house of Cornelius. Although they had heard that the Gentiles had received the Word of God, they were upset that the Law had been "violated."

In response, Peter related his vision, the vision of Cornelius and the moving of the Holy Spirit when the Gospel was shared. What happened next?

> When they heard these things they fell silent. And they
> glorified God, saying, "Then to the Gentiles also God has
> granted repentance that leads to life." Acts 11:18

Although we might question the underlying motivation of the circumcised believers, there is truly nothing wrong with what they did. It was important for people to understand what God was doing in and through the early church. We can look back and celebrate this incredible gift of a living and active Word that still speaks.

God gave His Word so that His people may know of His love and His will. It is the story of His historical dealings with His people. The main premise of the Bible is to reveal to us our need for God and His unconditional willingness to meet that need. We are a sinful people, incapable of accomplishing our own salvation. Jesus Christ was the means through which our salvation was granted. The Bible itself is a tool of accountability, exhorting us to press on.

> Therefore, since we are surrounded by so great a cloud
> of witnesses, let us also lay aside every weight, and sin
> which clings so closely, and let us run with endurance the
> race that is set before us . . . Hebrews 12: 1

In the Old Testament, the priests and prophets were used by God to hold the Israelites accountable. In the New Testament, the disciples were accountable to Jesus and to one another. Today, leaders are accountable to Jesus and should be accountable to one another.

Implementation will require accountability. On the front end of the planning process, establish a time line of accountability. Determine who is accountable to whom and an accepted mechanism for activating that accountability. Agree on a clear course of action as steps are completed *or* if steps are not completed. In most cases, building a system of mutually agreed upon checks and balances initially will keep and negative steps from needing to be used.

When Do We Make Adjustments To The Plan?

In light of what happened with Peter and Cornelius, you might anticipate that change is radical and frequent. That is potentially a very dangerous perspective.

In Acts fifteen, we read of a Council at Jerusalem. There was a dispute among believers as to the application of the Law and faith in Jesus Christ. Some were teaching that circumcision was a requirement after conversion. The Apostle Paul (see Galatians chapter two) was in strong opposition to Peter over the issue. Why?

A group of people claimed that obedience to the Law was required. They had reverted back to the familiar and legalistic ways of following God. It was the comfort of an old blanket as they enjoyed what they had known for so long.

They were going back to old habits. The Truth was being pushed aside as they sought to add requirements to the gift of grace.

In good plans, opportunities are built in for periodic evaluation, refinement and fine-tuning. Your purpose as a church will not change. It was given by Jesus Christ and is non-negotiable. (Verbiage can be changed but the underlying purpose does not.) *We are to make disciples, teaching them to follow Christ.*

Leaders can consider this illustration. If a person has poor eyesight, they can choose to wear glasses. The frames may change if the style changes, but they continue to wear glasses. At some point, they may switch to contacts. The need (*focus*) for eyesight to be corrected has not changed but they were able to switch to a different method to achieve positive results. In other words, the *form* through which it is being corrected has changed. Therefore, as leaders change (or even the pastor), the focus remains clear. Only the elimination of the need (corrective eye surgery) would signal a radical change in vision.

Consider the following principles to keep in place.

- Our vision should be a long-term proposition based on who our church is and the community in which we serve.

Unless there are major changes in either, our vision should be somewhat consistent.

- Objectives change as we accomplish the goals that we have established and move on to new possibilities as we fulfill our vision.

- Goals must always be specific, attainable, measurable and desirable.

- Strategies often must be refined depending on the underlying circumstances of our work. Even a Stradivarius needs to be properly tuned to make the best music!

As we keep our focus on the main target on the horizon, small course adjustments are always necessary. Fine-tuning should be just that. Plans, by and large, should be allowed to run their course. By staying the course, we will win the race marked out before us.

How Do We Keep The Process of Master Planning Alive?

In the Old Testament, the *Diasporas* were those Jewish people *scattered* as they were taken into captivity. In the New Testament, the first letter of Peter is addressed to God's strangers in the world who are "*diasporas*." The Greek word is commonly translated as "scattered." As we consider Peter's communication to the scattered believers in the region, we should see how a letter from an Apostle would help keep their faith alive.

The next few lines from Peter provide praise to God and encouragement for the people. There is a reminder of their eternal inheritance and the blessings that will be theirs as they are refined by fire. In many ways, it's a love letter, reminding them of their reasons for hope and joy and the promise of a great reunion!

God's Word is living and active. However, too often, we can read the epistles as if they are simple letters. While they are letters, we should consider the big picture of their inclusion in the canon of Scripture. These letters were communications in *real* time to *real* people in *real* places to provide guidance for a *real* and living faith. We need to read them in light of the context and culture so deeply ingrained within them.

Given the familial and tribal ties of the believers, this *scattering* would have been incredibly difficult from a societal perspective. In our global, internet-connected world, the richness of this personal connection can be lost when we don't think of the deepness of this extended parting. It's easy for us to imagine picking up a phone to call a friend or send a message. They didn't have these options so it was more difficult for them to keep relationship connections alive without being intentional.

But, if our connections are easier today, why does it seem our relationships so often die?

Where is this headed? To figure out how to keep the master planning process alive, let's first figure out how we can *keep relationships alive.*

Relationships stay alive in large part through communication. When counseling a couple, the first thing to do is check their communication. Marriages that work are marriages where the bride and groom keep talking, sharing and growing together—in spite of their individual imperfections.

Understand that our Groom is perfect. Jesus Christ is our spotless Savior (1st Peter 1:19). However, the Church, the Bride of Christ is not without her imperfections. Bluntly, the church is full of sinners—sinners saved by grace, but sinners nevertheless. As life happens, so do unexpected twists and turns in the life of the church.

As leaders and even pastors change, it can be very difficult to develop a plan that will be sustained for decades rather than just months. How do you build a master plan that will survive any leadership separation and the passage of time?

> "The leader should always have dreams he cannot complete and visions that will last far beyond his tenure. Then the mission is more important than the man. Then the people matter even when the next leader takes over. Then there is hope and not just history. Leaders who finish

well are not those who run the last race before the track
lights are turned off. Leaders who finish well are those
who pass the baton to their successors to run the next leg
of the race. Blessed are those who make their successors
succeed." *Leadership That Works*, Leith Anderson

The mission, vision and master plan should be bigger than
individuals. Your plan should capture the imagination and commitment of your congregation *for generations*. Understanding
who you are and what you stand for will ignite the fires of your
success for years and years and years. But we need to be sure to
communicate reminders of that hope.

Our hope is to be built on nothing less than Jesus Christ. He
is our sure foundation (1ˢᵗ Corinthians 3:11). Any pastor, leader
or church member must keep their feet firmly planted on that
rock. There may be changes to a plan, but our hope is the same—
for time and for eternity.

Let us *keep on* encouraging one another to draw closer to
our Heavenly Father. Let us *keep on* encouraging one another to
draw closer. Let us *keep on* encouraging one another to persevere. (Hebrews 10: 19–25)

What Will Be Our Greatest Barrier To Success?

In his book, *Hidden in Plain Sight*, pastor and author Mark Bu-
chanan presents a compelling vision for our successive growth
through in virtues listed in Peter's second letter. Our foundation
is faith. To that, we add goodness. To that, we add knowledge.
And so on . . .

As we add each virtue, the preceding virtue grows stronger
as well. In other words, if we add knowledge, we more quickly
recognize God's goodness. The more quickly we recognize
God's goodness, the deeper our faith in Him will become. This
is the process of spiritual growth that Christians refer to as
sanctification.

But this is a *process* . . .

We are being set apart from the world. We need to be committed to following Christ and growing in our faith. If we are disciples, we need to be committed disciples. We need to seek to grow in our understanding and in the practice of our faith. We need to seek to press forward in spite of opposition.

> Finally, be strong in the Lord and in the strength of his might. Put on the whole armor of God, that you may be able to stand against the schemes of the devil. For we do not wrestle against flesh and blood, but against the rulers, against the authorities, against the cosmic powers over this present darkness, against the spiritual forces of evil in the heavenly places. Ephesians 6: 10–12

A church on the edge of implementing a divinely inspired plan for changing the world for the Lord Jesus Christ is a serious and intimidating threat to the world of the comfortable. You must understand that, especially at this stage, there may be people who don't like change. There will be forces at work in the unseen realm seeking to do everything to keep God's plan from moving forward.

Our greatest barrier to success could be any number of visible or invisible things. But the way we combat those forces is to put on the armor of God. We need to be strong in Him and His mighty Power.

It's not our plan. It's *His*.
It's not our strength. It's *His*.
It's not our power. It's *His*.
And it's not our success. It's *His*.

Action Steps

1. Honestly, it is not difficult to gather a consensus in a church that changes need to be made. However, taking the initiative to implement these changes can be difficult. Consider the following questions individually and corporately.

a.   Where is this church in the planning process?

_____

_____

b.   Is this church serious about discerning God's plan for the church?

_____

_____

_____

c.   What do you need to do next to begin action?

_____

_____

_____

2.   Prayer is the ultimate key to success. Spend time in individual and corporate prayer over the Ten Components. Intentionally build a vital and healthy atmosphere of prayer surrounding these efforts. Remember to keep your prayer chain updated on the praises!

3.   Consider the Process of Renewal. How can your church be more intentional about energizing and renewing your church by planning events periodically to enhance your ministry?

_____

_____

_____

_____

_____

LRM is committed to serving the local church as it renews, motivates and equips men and women for ministry. We believe that renewal is a process. The church will experience healthy ministry and vital growth as members commit themselves to consistent and intentional levels of:

- Leadership Renewal and Development
- Congregational Renewal
- Mission, Vision and Strategy
- Resourcing and Equipping

God does not want our second best. How can we do more to glorify God going forward?

One More Chapter?

Wait a minute!

One more chapter?

Why?

As the church has been studied throughout history, it has become clear that churches have vision and life cycles. The gruesomeness of a dead church is revealed in stark contrast when a church comes alive.

When a church is new (or renewed), those in the church are reaching out to those immersed in spiritual chaos. Focused on self alone, the individuals in this realm are headed to eternal death in hell. The church is doing everything in its power to reach out to these people who are being called by God and show them the message of grace and truth so that they will become disciples living in the realm of spiritual order.

In this area, the Holy Spirit effects life change in the hearts of these individuals. Vital growth occurs in their lives and in the life of the church. To assist with this growth, the church will develop organizational structures. However, with these structures *can* (not will, but can) come a blockage called "THE RUT."

With this blockage, the Holy Spirit is unintentionally pushed aside as man becomes the primary agent in the church. Motivational death occurs, as programs become the focus over ministry. Programs are not bad things, but when they become institutionalized, ministry is lost. Creativity and excitement are lost until vision is renewed.

Renewed vision is the key.

As we discussed in the introduction to the last chapter, Peter experienced a restoration in his relationship with the risen Christ. He was called back to feed the sheep. Peter's three denials were literally erased as Jesus called him back three times. "The Rock" was restored in his relationship and affirmed in his ability to lead.

We need to be renewed in our relationship with our Savior.

When most campers wake up on a cold morning, the first thing they do is to stir the ashes and rebuild the fire. Our churches need to have a time in which we can call back the "drifting sheep" to a renewed focus of serving God. This is not a trivial time to simply throw together. This is a passionate time to stoke the fire and encourage the walk.

And remember that sometimes when we walk in life, we step on nails. I grew up spending time on construction sites with my father and experienced that pain much, much too often. Honestly? That was *nothing*.

Two thousand years ago, our Savior had nails driven into

His flesh.

His hands and feet were pierced.

His blood was poured out on the ground.

He did that for me.

He did that for you.

Those very same nails that were used to kill our King should be used to drive you to build a church that will glorify Him in all that is done. How is your fire today? Do you need the ashes stirred in your heart so that you can break out of your rut and serve the King anew?

This is important.

We have an assurance that God is at work in and through us.

Now to him who is able to do far more abundantly than all that we ask or think, according to the power at work within us, to him be glory in the church and in Christ

Jesus throughout all generations, forever and ever. Amen. Ephesians 3: 20–21

There must be a foundational assumption embraced. God loves you. He loves your church. He has developed a plan for your church. He has provided you with all of the tools necessary to accomplish that plan for Him. The church's job is to discover the plan, develop the gifts and deploy its members to service—and trust in God.

Don't waste time.
Don't make excuses.
Just do it.

There is no Plan B.

Accept it.
Work with it.
Thank God for it.

For this reason I bow my knees before the Father, from whom every family in heaven and on earth is named, that according to the riches of his glory he may grant you to be strengthened with power through his Spirit in your inner being, so that Christ may dwell in your hearts through faith—that you, being rooted and grounded in love, may have strength to comprehend with all the saints what is the breadth and length and height and depth, and to know the love of Christ that surpasses knowledge, that you may be filled with all the fullness of God.

Ephesians 3:14–19

Appendix One

Sample Master Planning Worksheet

INSTRUCTIONS: DISTRIBUTE TO DESIGNATED leadership groups. Under each of the following six categories, prayerfully evaluate and list specific items that answer the questions.

1. Needs: What needs do the members of our church feel especially burdened by and uniquely qualified to meet?

   a. _____

   b. _____

   c. _____

   d. _____

   e. _____

2. Milestones: What unique events or ministry moments has this church been able to do through God's Power over our church's history?

   a. _____

   b. _____

   c. _____

   d. _____

   e. _____

3. Resources: With what resources (including people, finances, facility, etc...) has God equipped our church? (This is not what you want. It is what you have!)

   a. _____

   b. _____

   c. _____

   d. _____

   e. _____

4. Roadblocks: What are potential hindrances to moving forward?

   a. _____

   b. _____

   c. _____

   d. _____

   e. _____

5. Perceptions: What are some key internal and external perceptions about the church? What do people think about the call of this church to minister?

   a. _____

   b. _____

   c. _____

   d. _____

   e. _____

6. Dreams: If there were not obstacles, what would you do? If finances were unlimited, what would you do? Dream BIG!

    a. _____

    b. _____

    c. _____

    d. _____

    e. _____

Appendix Two

INSTRUCTIONS: AS A LEADERSHIP team, discuss the various ministries listed below. Place a mark in the appropriate column as you perceive the current ministry status.

		Added	Improved	Increased	Eliminated
A.	Separate youth ministry				
B.	Separate college ministry				
C.	Separate singles ministry				
D.	Separate couples ministry				
E.	Separate divorce ministry				
F.	Separate ministry to families				
G.	Saturday worship				
H.	Sunday eve. service				

I.	Week night service				
J.	Small Groups				
K.	Prayer/Healing service				
L.	Evangelism/visitation				
M.	Prayer ministry				
N.	Individual discipleship				
O.	Bus ministry				
P.	Choir/music ministry				
Q.	Full-time counseling				
R.	Mother's day out				
S.	Media ministry				
T.	Shut-in/hospital ministry				
U.	Foreign missions				
V.	Church planting				
W.	Christian school				
X.	Older Adult ministry				
Y.	Other:				
Z.	Other:				

Appendix Three

Evaluating the Physical Aspects of Your Church

INSTRUCTIONS: As OBJECTIVELY AS possible, approach this worksheet as with "outside eyes." If you were visiting for the first time, what would you see? If you question your objectivity, consider having a third party from outside the church walk with you to mark as appropriate.

	High Quality	Average	Needs Improvement
First Impression Factors:			
● Exterior			
○ Landscaping	_____	_____	_____
○ Condition of parking lot	_____	_____	_____
○ Visitor parking	_____	_____	_____
● Interior			
○ Entry Points	_____	_____	_____
○ Greeters	_____	_____	_____
○ Signage	_____	_____	_____
○ Restrooms	_____	_____	_____

- o Nursery /
  Childcare ___ ___ ___
- o Sunday School
  rooms ___ ___ ___
- Worship
  - o Entry points ___ ___ ___
  - o Atmosphere ___ ___ ___
  - o Seating ___ ___ ___
  - o Music ___ ___ ___
  - o Announcements ___ ___ ___
- Information Distribution / Capturing
  - o First-time visitor
    registration ___ ___ ___
  - o Follow-up
    Program ___ ___ ___
  - o Repeat guest ___ ___ ___
  - o Third-time repeat
    guest ___ ___ ___
- Integration Methods
  - o New member
    class schedule ___ ___ ___
  - o Sunday School ___ ___ ___
  - o Small group /
    Care group ___ ___ ___
  - o Men's / Women's
    Ministry ___ ___ ___

- Web Site (this is a new physical "*outside*" impression point!) _____ _____ _____
- Other

  ○ _____ _____ _____ ____

  ○ _____ _____ _____ ____

  ○ _____ _____ _____ ____

  ○ _____ _____ _____ ____

  ○ _____ _____ _____ ____